Graham Handley MA PhD

Brodie's Notes on William Shakespeare's

Sonnets

Pan Books London and Sydney

First published 1978 by Pan Books Ltd
Cavaye Place, London SW10 9PG
3 4 5 6 7 8 9

ISBN 0 330 50143 7
Filmset in Great Britain by
Northumberland Press Ltd, Gateshead, Tyne and Wear
Printed and bound by
Richard Clay (The Chaucer Press) Ltd, Bungay, Suffolk

Contents

To the student

A close reading of the sonnets is the student's primary task. These Notes will help to increase your understanding and appreciation of the sonnets, and to stimulate *your own* thinking about them: *the Notes are in no way intended as a substitute* for a thorough knowledge of the poetry.

The author and his work

Surprisingly little is known about the life of our greatest dramatist, whose major sequence of poems is the subject of the following pages. The little we do know is derived mainly from brief references to his name in legal and other formal documents. He was born in Stratford-on-Avon and, though the exact date of his birth is unknown (23 April is merely traditional), there is a record of his having been christened William on 26 April 1564. He was the third child of John Shakespeare, a man variously described as glover and whittawer (tanner), and more doubtfully as wool-dealer, farmer and butcher. Until about 1578, when his business began to decline, John Shakespeare was a notable figure in Stratford; and it is probable that William was educated at Stratford Grammar School, where he would have learned the 'small Latin and less Greek' for which Jonson gave him credit.

At the age of eighteen Shakespeare married Anne Hathaway, a woman eight years older than he; and by 1585 three children had been born of the marriage. It is in this year that Shakespeare is thought to have left Stratford for London. Tradition has it that his departure was due to trouble over deer-stealing in the grounds of Sir Thomas Lucy, but one theory is that he left with a band of strolling players (The Queen's Players), who visited Stratford in 1585. Others are that he taught in a country school, or served as a soldier – military and scholastic images abound in the plays.

It is just possible that his (reputedly unhappy) marriage to Anne Hathaway precipitated Shakespeare's departure from his native town. Whether his wife and children ever lived with him in London is not known for certain, but it seems unlikely – and for eight years we hear nothing of him. However, in 1592 a pamphlet was published by Robert Greene, playwright and wit, which speaks of Shakespeare in a roundabout fashion as actor and playwright.

Plague caused the theatres to be closed in 1593, and on their reopening the following year we know that Shakespeare was a member of the Lord Chamberlain's Company (known after the accession of James I as the King's Men), and it is probable that he stayed with this company for the rest of his career, writing plays for it and acting with it in the various theatres. His connection with the company must have brought him considerable financial reward, for we know that in 1596 his father, presumably aided by his successful son, applied to the College of Heralds for the right to assume a family coat of arms, and in the following year the playwright purchased New Place, one of the largest houses in Stratford. Although the house is no longer there, the foundations can be seen, and the garden is open to the public.

As his fortunes prospered, Shakespeare bought shares in two theatres, the Globe built in 1599, and the Blackfriars built in 1596. He would, therefore, in addition to his pay as actor and writer, have received his share of the profits on these investments. Thus in 1611, when still under fifty, Shakespeare retired to his native town a wealthy man. However, he seems to have kept up a connection with London: in 1615 he was concerned in a legal dispute over the purchase of a house in Blackfriars. Shakespeare died in Stratford-on-Avon in April 1616, survived by his wife and two daughters, and he was buried in the parish church. It is not intended to give here a list of his plays, or to describe his dramatic achievements, since these are too well known to need chronology. But the student may be interested to know that in addition to the 154 sonnets which are thought to be his, his other poetry consists of *Venus and Adonis* and *The Rape of Lucrece* (published in 1593 and 1594 respectively, and both dedicated to the Earl of Southampton), and perhaps *The Phoenix and the Turtle* and *A Lover's Complaint*.

Further reading

Shakespeare's Sonnets, ed. W. G. Ingram, T. Redpath (Hodder & Stoughton paperback)

New Shakespeare Sonnets, ed. J. Dover Wilson (CUP)

Themes and Variations in Shakespeare's Sonnets, J. B. Leishman (Hutchinson)

Shakespeare and the sonnet: a critical introduction

The Elizabethan Age is the golden age of the English sonnet: although its reign was brief, it remains one of the outstanding literary genres of its time. The sonnet originated in Italy, and its popularity in the period can be accounted for by the newly awakened interest in Italian literature. There were several influential Italian sonnet writers, but it was above all the formative influence of Francesco Petrarch (1304–74) that prevailed, and was adapted in England to Elizabethan conventions. In his sonnets Petrarch expressed his undying love for 'Laura': she was the type, the ideal, of womanhood, and above all the unattainable object of love. Petrarch's English imitators responded to the sonnet's strictness of form, while making their own experiments within it. (Italian has a greater facility of rhyme than English.) Petrarch's sonnets were indeed circumscribed: the first eight lines (the octave), rhymed abba abba, though the following six lines (the sestet) in fact allowed for a slight variation in rhyme scheme. The first eight lines carried the definition or statement of the sonnet's theme, while the extensions or working out were to be found in the sestet.

In the English sonnets, the poet is male, adoring, suffering, often plaintive – unrequited love being the most common theme. Ingenuity is the key, but often it fails to unlock the heart: all too frequently the Elizabethan sonnet is an exercise in the use of 'conceits' – the exploration of love and its expression in terms of a particular imagery. It should be noted in this context, however, that an easy colloquialism early makes a (sporadic) appearance in the English sonnets.

In fact, the sonnet in England was to grow far beyond the confines of the Italian convention, and this appears soon after Shakespeare's death in the sonnets of *John Donne* (1572–1631). Donne rough-hews the form to fit his burning religious thought. Later in the seventeenth century *Milton* (1608–74) turns to the sonnet for the expression of political as well as personal emotion – witness 'On the Late Massacre in Piedmont', for example, the sonnet on his vision of his dead wife and, even more moving, that on his own blindness.

In the eighteenth century the sonnet tends, on the whole to become overshadowed; but with the advent of the Romantic movement, late in the eighteenth century, it once more increases in individuality. *Wordsworth* (1770–1850) both defends and practises the sonnet: students might look at the remarkable sonnet in which he views sleeping London from Westminster Bridge (1802); the sonnet addressed to Milton, 'Nuns fret not at their convent's narrow room' (a sonnet commenting *on* the sonnet); or the poignant expression of love and loss to be found in 'Surprised by joy, impatient as the wind'. *Shelley* (1792–1822) wrote 'Ozymandias', and that terrible indictment 'England 1819' which begins, 'An old, mad, blind, despised and dying King'. *Keats*'s (1795–1821) genius is early found in the sonnet 'On First Looking Into Chapman's Homer', while his tragic sense of imminent death is seen in 'Bright Star, would I were steadfast as thou art', among his other fine sonnets.

The Victorians sometimes turned to the sonnet, and here perhaps the most famous sequence is the exquisite *Sonnets from the Portuguese* by *Elizabeth Barrett Browning* (1806–61) containing the unforgettable 'How shall I love thee? Let me count the ways'. *Dante Gabriel Rossetti* (1828–82) wrote many sonnets, (in addition to translating Italian sonneteers); those of *Gerard Manley Hopkins* (1844–89) are reminiscent of Donne in their religious passion and their metrical irregularity.

Many poets of the twentieth century have appropriated the sonnet; for instance, with the outbreak of World War I in 1914 *Rupert Brooke* (1887–1915) was moved to write the patriotic and immensely popular 'If I should die, think only this of me'. Nearer our own time, *W. H. Auden* (1907–73), with typical idiosyncratic liberalism, produced a sequence called *Sonnets from China.* The modern sonnet often differs widely from the Elizabethan conventional structure: breaks may occur in the line; the lines themselves may vary in length; rhymes may be used or ignored; and the divisions of octave and sestet may be either observed or neglected.

But here we are concerned with the sixteenth century, and the prime influences on Shakespeare. The earliest exponents of the sonnet in England are *Sir Thomas Wyatt* (1503–42) and *the Earl of Surrey* (1517–47); they are broadly Petrarchan in practice. Wyatt goes beyond that, however, by sometimes treating of themes other than love; Surrey heralds the Shakespearean rhyme-scheme. All Shakespeare's sonnets end with a couplet, and virtually all of them have the rhyme-scheme used by Surrey – abab cdcd efef gg – in three quatrains and a clinching couplet. *Spenser* wrote fine sonnets, but (apart from Shakespeare), the greatest sonneteer among the later Elizabethans is probably *Sir Philip Sidney* (1554–86). He was almost certainly the major influence on Shakespeare, and his sequence *Astrophel and Stella* was published in 1591, some five years after his death. The sequence draws markedly on the theme of unrequited love, in images which are rarely original, often trite, but sometimes delicately and deftly handled in the working out of the fashionable 'conceits'. The epigrammatic tension of the couplet was further developed; and the interested student will pay particular attention to the sonnet which begins, 'With how sad steps, O Moon, thou climb'st the skies', for here the sestet ends in a questioning couplet, and questions are a prominent feature of Shakespeare's own technique.

During the 1590s a number of books and sonnets were published, often addressed to a real or an imaginary lady-love, so that Shakespeare is at once part of the convention which, by his individual treatment, he often transcends. But while we may note in passing the dates and achievements of his contemporaries, the dates of composition of Shakespeare's own sonnets remain a mystery. Francis Meres, in *Palladis Tamia*

(1598), makes a reference to Shakespeare as both dramatist and poet, and indicates that some of the 'sug'red Sonnets' were known and admired. Two were published, though in somewhat different form, in *The Passionate Pilgrim* in 1599, and these two are well advanced in the sequence as we have it (numbers 138 and 144). There is a little, equivocal evidence to indicate that one or two sonnets may refer to particular events. The most commonly accepted view is that the date of composition was somewhere in the 1590s, and later rather than earlier.

We are not concerned here with the dating, but with the sonnets as literature. It will be apparent from our later commentary on the individual sonnets that certain *themes and language* (particularly *imagery*) and certain *techniques* are central to our appreciation of them. Shakespeare, as has been said, used the Surrey-type adaptation of the Petrarchan sonnet; this made for *unforced fluency*, *word-play*, *wit*, *double-entendres*, various types of *innuendo* and, above all, the *epigrammatic, climaxing couplet*. These are the main elements, but in addition there are often *internal rhymes, groups or clusters of images* (from those of Nature to legal terminology), and a clear division into sequences which, though capable of subdivision (and rearrangement by scholarly editors intent on proving a point) may be summarized thus:

Sonnets 1–126 To the friend.
Sonnets 127–52 To the dark lady.
Sonnets 153–4 'Cupid's Fire'.

It was in 1609 that Thomas Thorpe the publisher brought out the sonnets, with the dedication which the student of these notes should read (most editions of the sonnets print it), and around which so much basic detective work has centred. Speculation as to whether the young man addressed is the Earl of Southampton or the Earl of Pembroke, or even some other claimant, still continues. For the purpose of this study, the theories surrounding these two or any others are ignored, as indeed are theories that deal with the order of the sonnets; one is forced to acknowledge here that Thorpe's order may not be Shakespeare's, though, with reservations, it has satisfied most scholars. Many read the sonnets as a continuous story, but even this is not necessary to their appreciation. It may be that they are conveniently interconnected by theme and image, art and artifice, but there need be no basis in autobiographical fact.

The practice of poetry was an exercise undertaken by fashionable and cultivated young men of the Elizabethan period. The student is therefore advised to treat the poems for what they are – splendid verse for the most part, observing and yet transcending particular conventions – and to work out *the main themes, patterns of imagery, sentiments and particular conceits* that Shakespeare employs.

It is all too easy to get so caught up with the *background* to a writer that one forgets the *foreground*, which is the works themselves. It will be obvious from the poem-by-poem commentary that follows that there are certain overall themes: praise of the friend (in order to retain his patronage?) and the employment of a range of imagery that exemplifies this theme. The poet's friend and the sentiments he feels from him strike one as real. The *friend's physical beauty and nobility of character*, his generosity and his graciousness, are seen (when we have read all the sonnets) *in contrast to the dark lady, who is physically unattractive, promiscuous; she represents the obverse side of love*, that which is degrading rather than ennobling. Themes include the *invocation to the friend to perpetuate himself* by marrying and having an heir; reflections on his kindness, though he is sometimes self-indulgent and wanton; his integrity of character; and his superiority. The fact that a man is the recipient of the first 126 poems, while it may prove distasteful to some, cannot in any way undermine the quality of the sequence or the verbal mastery it displays.

Sonnet 20 exemplifies both the fascination and the enigma of the sonnets; it is at once the treasure-house and the burial-ground of many commentators, for the expression 'master-mistress' has been the subject of much critical commentary and explanation. In fact, the phrase strikes the note of so many of the sonnets, a man addressing a master (patron, master of his heart) in the terms of adoration and romantic expression he would use for a mistress. This involves the onset of jealousy (of a rival poet), and moreover the story of his 'friend's' affair with the dark lady in the later sequence. The dark lady too has been the focal point of interest, both scholarly and salacious, though it seems reasonable to assume that the inspiration of many of 'her' sonnets is a revulsion *against* the convention – the love-adoration-purity hallmark of the Petrarchan mode – rather than the deliberate evocation of a particular person. Sonnet 130 is a remarkable expression of anti-Petrarchan sentiment, since all the conventional epithets of praise devoted to the hair, the eyes, the voice, are turned on end in a masterly satirical attack on the accepted mode. Equally, the identity of the rival poet is also a mystery, though many critics have plumped for that celebrated translator of Homer who so inspired Keats, George Chapman.

Linked to the central theme of the early sonnets – *the begetting of an heir* – is one which deals with *the effects of Time*, for this is the perennial concern of the sequence in one emphasis or another. Many of the sonnets are concerned with the overcoming of time through the agency of the poet, who will always preserve the beauty and grace of the young man through the immortality of his verse. This has its obverse side too, for on occasion the poet feels his own apathy and the inadequacy of his language to achieve his immortality, particularly when it is seen against the writings of his rivals. In fact, the sonnets are a study of the *mind's ebb and flow*, whether this be charted by convention or by whim, or whether the unravelling of a particular conceit (*Nature*, legal *imagery*, *ships and the sea*, for example). *Immortality* for the beloved is sometimes paralleled by immortality for the poet, so that he also has transcended time. The pendulum of mood swings yet again when the poet writes of *absence*: his friend has forsaken him, or been absent from him, or he has been absent from the friend; and the poet describes the thoughts and emotions to which these absences give rise. The sonnet is well fitted for *changes of mood* and *emotional about-turns*, as witness the famous sonnet by Michael Drayton (1563–1631), beginning, 'Since there's no help, come let us kiss and part,/Nay, I have done: you get no more of me', but changing to a more conciliatory and hopeful mood in the last six lines:

> Now at the last gasp of Love's latest breath,
> When his pulse failing, Passion speechless lies,
> When Faith is kneeling by his bed of death,
> And Innocence is closing up his eyes,
> Now if thou would'st, when all have given him over,
> From death to life, thou might'st him yet recover.

In Shakespeare's sonnets there is sometimes expressed the fear that he has lost his love, not merely physically but in the spirit as well. In the dark-lady sequence love has become lust, and the ensuing corruption embraces the poet's soul. Both sequences (the fair friend, and the dark lady) share a constantly recurring *reference to Nature*, while the *imagery* also includes *references to astrology, to acting, to painting, to war*.

These are a fraction of the poetic range, which includes attacks on false refinements of style; and these remarks can convey little of the depth of insight Shakespeare achieved in his use and manipulation of convention. It is hoped that our summaries and notes will provide the student with the full thematic range and presentation essential to something like a full appreciation of Shakespeare's art. In all critical appraisal, the text is the thing, and each sequence of the sonnets must be considered as a whole.

There are many editions of the sonnets, and these often keep (as we do here) to the order of Thomas Thorpe's 1609 Quarto. (John Benson in 1640 put out an edition rearranging them, among other alterations.) The student should be alive to variant readings, and should try, cautiously, to link the sonnets – themes, language, word-play – to the plays. This would be to encompass the whole art of Shakespeare, who transcended form in the sonnets, and life in the plays, his immortality secure in both from 'Time's fell hand'.

Sonnet summaries and textual notes

Sonnet 1

This sonnet embodies a favourite theme of Shakespeare's – one much employed in Elizabethan sonnets generally – the idea of the heir perpetuating the parent's talents and beauty. Here the poet upbraids his friend for being his own worst enemy, and self-destructive in his attitude. He goes on to praise the friend's beauty, urging him not to 'eat the world's due' but to pay that due, i.e. provide an heir. The imagery is of nature and of fire, and these concepts are in turn reinforced by that of appetite and miserliness. (The student might contrast the Puritan reaction to this in Milton's *Comus*, lines 706–99 where the falsity of the argument is attacked.)

rose Flush, bloom, youth.
contracted to i.e. wedded to.
self-substantial i.e. consuming yourself, egoistic.
famine . . . abundance A favourite contrast from nature.
only herald i.e. the pre-eminent one.
thine own bud i.e. not fully developed. The implication is: not complete until an heir has been produced.
churl . . . niggarding Miser . . . hoarding. Note the length of 'niggarding', implying a long time of doing nothing but hoarding.
Pity the world The last two lines urge the friend to give to the world (not the grave), its 'due' (by leaving behind an heir).

Sonnet 2

The idea of having a child to perpetuate your own youth when you are middle-aged is the main theme of this sonnet; the couplet suggests that the blood will be warmed and youth renewed. Time is seen as 'beseiging'; and the couplet has the balance of antithesis (new . . . old . . . warm . . . cold).

forty winters i.e. when you are forty years old.
beseige ... trenches Often Shakespeare's language has a cumulative effect, as here – the onset of age is compared to the military reduction of a town.
proud livery Showy appearance.
so gaz'd on i.e. admired.
tatter'd weed Tattered garment.
treasure i.e. gain.
lusty Full of vigour.
all-eating ... thriftless Degrading and profitless, because centred in *self* only.
use The implication is 'good use' or 'profit'.
sum my count Balance my accounts (justify my existence).
by succession Note the legal term, one of many used in the sonnets, and a recurring motif with Shakespeare.

Sonnet 3

(Note the quickening of tempo in relation to the more stately movement of the first two sonnets.)

The now familiar theme of renewal, now expressed through the mirror – marking the ephemeral victory of time – but with fertility images of harvest in dynamic contrast. Just as now his friend's prime reflects that of his own mother; so in his age must he be able to see the epitome of himself in his child, for otherwise he will die totally, and there will be no living memory of him.

thy glass Mirror.
should form another i.e. beget a child.
fresh repair Good condition.
beguile i.e. delude or cheat.
unbless i.e. (you) do not bless (by giving her a child).
unear'd womb Not ploughed (a fertility image). The harvest would obviously be the child.
tillage ... husbandry This continues the above image with the idea of preparing the soil properly, that is, fertility in the sexual sense. But 'husbandry' suggests 'husband' (a part-pun) – an indication to the friend to marry and procreate.

the tomb ... posterity i.e. who is prepared to make his self-conceit his own grave, to stop himself perpetuating his kind.
glass Mirror as above, and therefore reflection.
windows His aged eyes, and the sight of his child who reflects his own youth.
remember'd Unremembered in any child.

Sonnet 4

This time use is made of the law, and of money – lending, borrowing, miserliness – as the natural result of beauty's legacy. The sonnet is close-knit, and unified by its legal terminology, with cross-reference to surrounding sonnets.

Unthrifty Wasteful.
legacy ... bequest i.e. What is legally left is compared to what is 'naturally' left to one's descendants, i.e. beauty.
gives ... lend The implication is that the 'friend' is loaned the beauty he has, and by the law of nature he must pass it on through procreation.
frank Generous. If there is a sexual connotation, one could compare that bitter couplet of Pope, 'chaste to her husband, frank to all beside'.
free This also means 'generous'. (Nature, being generous herself, lends to those who themselves are generous.)
niggard See note to Sonnet 1.
largess Gifts, rewards freely bestowed.
Profitless usurer Wasteful moneylender.
use Squander.
yet canst not live i.e. yet you cannot gain benefit.
traffic Business.
deceive Swindle.
when nature calls thee i.e. when it is your time to die.
acceptable audit (What) balanced account.
Thy unus'd beauty The last two lines mean 'What is not invested will be buried with you, but if you had invested it the legacy would have its own executor (i.e. in the form of an heir)'.

Sonnet 5

The theme is here further developed to embrace the ravages of time, extended through parallels with summer (youth) and winter (age) in nature. The octave runs on into the sestet, which expresses the idea that summer's essence remains as a perfume (though the flowers that produced it have been frosted over), a memory of what was; the simple analogy between what is left of summer and what he should leave from the summer of his life – an heir – is, to use Shakespeare's image, 'distill'd' in the couplet.

gentle work i.e. refined.
The lovely gaze This refers to the object of the gaze – the friend.
unfair . . . fairly Note the word-play, a favourite device, 'unfair' is a negative verb, probably meaning 'to take away beauty'.
summer . . . winter Youth . . . age.
confounds Destroys.
Sap check'd i.e. growth stopped.
distillation Essence, perfume.
A liquid prisoner Perhaps a continued reference to the imprisonment entailed by frost, but certainly the idea of essence or perfume in a bottle is meant.
Beauty's effect with beauty The word-play again, meaning here (If there were no perfume) the effect of what was beautiful would be lost when that beauty disappeared.
Leese Lose. The outward appearance goes, but the essence remains – another plea to perpetuate by procreation. Note the exquisite alliteration here.

Sonnet 6

A continuation of the theme and imagery of the previous poem, with a tortuous passage in the octave which runs into the sestet. The opening is a fine personification which underlines the identification of Nature and man, but the play on the word 'ten' is less successful, more commonplace than elevated. The reference to 'self-kill'd' and 'self-will'd', though spaced in the poem, embodies the poet's fear that his friend will not act to perpetuate himself, but will remain locked in his own self-sufficiency.

ragged hand Rough (passage of time).
deface Spoil.
distill'd Carrying on from the previous poem, it means here 'your essence' (a child).
vial Perfume is kept in a bottle, but the image here obviously refers to the womb.
treasure Used verbally, meaning 'fill'.
self-kill'd i.e. before love of self stops procreation.
use ... usury Punning, or at least half-punning. The meaning here is that the friend is free to beget an heir, the wife being made happy by bearing him children (being prepared to 'pay the willing loan'). There is much play on 'pay', and the 'ten' refers to the degree of interest, which is seen here as an image for happiness.
refigur'd Reproduced an exact likeness.
self-will'd i.e. set in your own ways, obstinate.
conquest Inheritance – here again a legal term.
make worms thine heir i.e. feeding on the body in the grave.

Sonnet 7

The comparison sustaining the theme here is with the sun and its daily journey – with the bluntest statement so far in the couplet.

orient East.
gracious God-given and majestic.
his burning head Personification of the 'light' (the sun).
under eye i.e. each eye below (from the earth).
Serving Paying due homage to him.
steep-up heavenly hill i.e. the sheer sky.
in his middle age i.e. his height (noon).
Attending on his golden pilgrimage i.e. waiting upon his

journey (but note the spiritual associations present from the first line of the poem).

highmost pitch The zenith.

with weary car Phoebus, the sun-god, drove a chariot, hence the reference here.

'fore duteous i.e. hitherto doing their duty by worshipping the sun.

converted Turned.

tract Here in the sense of 'path'.

outgoing Outlasting your own prime, your peak.

Unlook'd on (Like the sun) you will disappear unnoticed.

Sonnet 8

Here the theme is developed, so to speak, through music, 'the true concord of well-tuned sounds' being compared to family harmony with father, mother and child.

Music to hear An elliptical way of saying 'You are music when you speak'.

Sweets ... sweets ... joy ... joy A rather sugary way of saying that happiness is in harmony with happiness, or perhaps that beauty begets beauty.

receiv'st not gladly i.e. which you find dull.

thine annoy Your own ennui (lack of occupation or interest, boredom).

true concord i.e. harmony.

unions married i.e. in tune.

sweetly chide Gently blame.

who confounds ... bear By remaining celibate you destroy the roles you should play (obviously of husband and father). But there is a continuation of the musical image.

one string Probably of a lute, where the strings echo each other. Note, too, the play on the word 'husband'.

Who all in one The harmony of family life.

thou single wilt prove none i.e. you will disappear, die out, if you remain single.

Sonnet 9

The same theme, but this time with a direct invocation to the friend. The word-play (particularly on 'world') is facile, and the absence of the customary imagery somehow diminishes the quality and the overall effect of this poem, which seems to be much more a verbal exercise than the others.

for fear to wet i.e. for fear that you will die and leave a weeping widow.
issueless shalt hap i.e. if it so happens that you die without heirs.
wail i.e. bewail, mourn (your passing).
makeless i.e. deprived of a mate.
still Forever.
private widow i.e. the ordinary widow, as distinct from the world which is the friend's widow.
By children's eyes i.e. seeing in her children's eyes the memorial of her husband.
unthrift Wastrel.
beauty's waste Beauty is wasted (worn) by the passing of time.
unus'd ... user The 'usual' word-play, with usury in mind, and the theme here 'wasting'.
murderous shame commits i.e. kills himself (since he does not perpetuate himself in a child).

Sonnet 10

Again this opens with a direct statement, an indictment of selfishness in the form of an accusation – that the friend loves himself and nobody else. Through the octave the poet pursues the theme of self-destruction in his friend, but the sestet has all the softness of the appeal to change hate to love, an urging of the friend to 'Be as thy presence is, gracious and kind'. The harsh opening lines provide a fine contrast with the plea that characterizes the final section and concludes in the couplet.

For shame deny i.e. deny it if you can, to your own shame.
unprovident Wasteful.
murderous hate Note the extreme nature of the image, a reinforcement of the harshness of tone at the beginning.
thou stick'st not i.e. you don't hesitate to.
beauteous roof i.e. outward appearance, physical beauty.
ruinate i.e. to waste or despoil.
Which to repair i.e. to make new again (by having a child in your own likeness).
hate ... love Note the effect of the contrast and the change of tone in the poet.
gracious See note p.21 for the full associations of this word.
Make thee another self The implication is that 'if you love me [the poet] you will do what I say, so that your own beauty will live on in the child you beget'.

Sonnet 11

Here there is a clear division between the first quatrain of the octave and the rest of the poem. In that first section the focus is on the benefit of procreation, but the theme is developed in the rest of the poem: that it should be reserved for those who are beautiful, and thus have something worthwhile to leave (i.e. the image of themselves). The concluding couplet uses the image of a seal or stamp and its subsequent reproduction as the equivalent of procreation.

As fast as thou shalt wane Even as you grow old so will you be renewed in your child.
youngly While you are young.
convertest See note p.21. Here it means 'leave', 'turn away from'.
Herein i.e. in having a child.
the times should cease Man would stop multiplying.
would make the world away i.e. would be the sum total of life.
for store i.e. worth reproducing or breeding.
whom she best endow'd Those whom Nature made the most beautiful (were also given the greatest vitality for procreation).

Which bounteous gift ... bounty Which generous gift you should use generously (i.e. the gift of being able to reproduce yourself by having a son).

her seal The stamp from which the impression is taken. ('She' is nature.)

print more The implication here is not just one child, but a number.

Sonnet 12

This presents the themes so far advanced, with the passage of time the main focus, seen in Nature and her seasons and in man, whose only 'defence' against time is to make another in his own image. The familiar image of 'Time's scythe' is employed for death, but lines 3 to 8 contain vivid and realistic images.

the brave day The implication is of strength and boldness.

hideous night Fearful darkness.

sable curls o'er-silvered all with white i.e. black hair become white with age, a warning to the friend.

barren of leaves Again the reference is to the ageing year (the autumn of life, if you like), but 'barren' carries its own warning.

erst Formerly.

canopy Cover, protect.

girded up in sheaves i.e. the gathering in of the harvest.

Borne on the bier The latter is generally the movable stand of the funeral, but here it is the cart. The death images obviously symbolize sterility or barrenness in man.

the wastes of time i.e. (that you) will be one of those whom time 'wastes' or destroys.

sweets and beauties i.e. in nature (flowers etc).

do themselves forsake i.e. are forced to abandon their own beauty with the passing of time – the changing of the seasons.

Time's scythe This is a commonplace, but here obviously grows out of the harvest imagery.

Save breed, to brave him i.e. a child or children to challenge Time. Note the heavy alliteration conveying the *power* of procreation.

Sonnet 13

The theme is here explored again through a series of repetitions, word-play, contrasts, the central image towards the end comparing the body to a house which has fallen into 'decay' when it might have been prevented by 'husbandry in honour', which is to be equated with acting to beget a child. The task is to unravel the pronouns (you, yourself) which are played on continually through the running alliteration, so that the whole has more the effect of an ingenious exercise than the preceding sonnets.

you are/No longer yours than you Complex word-play; it appears to mean that you are only yourself for as long as your body lives.

this coming end i.e. death.

your sweet semblance i.e. in the image of yourself, a child.

which you hold in lease/Find no determination Specialized legal imagery again, as in one or two of the earlier sonnets, 'lease' refers to the 'beauty' of the body – leasehold for life – and 'determination' means the winding up or conclusion of an estate. The appropriateness of the image will be obvious.

Your self again i.e. in the presence of your heir.

so fair a house Continuing the property image, the analogy, with the 'house' being the beauty of the friend.

husbandry in honour i.e. procreation, 'good management' of yourself by the begetting of a child.

winter's day Again the oblique reference is to the onset of age.

barren rage This has led to readings of 'ravage' for 'rage', but it may merely mean the complete unproductiveness of death, or that not to procreate is to experience a 'living death'.

Oh none but unthrifts Oh, nobody but wasteful, improvident people (behave so irresponsibly as not to beget a child).

You had a father Note the economy of the couplet.

Sonnet 14

Here the theme switches with considerable ingenuity to the stars and fortune or fate, returning inevitably to the 'eyes' of the friend (the 'stars' that shine for the poet), though again there is play on the words 'store' and 'convert'. The references to the stars imply 'forecasting', and here the poet 'forecasts' the birth of the beautiful heir or the simple end of his friend's life. The summary seems commonplace, but the treatment is brilliantly balanced.

my judgement pluck i.e. do I deduce.
I have astronomy Strictly, 'astrology', the art of judging the supposed influence of the stars on human affairs.
dearths Perhaps 'famines'.
seasons' quality i.e. what kind of spring or summer or harvest.
to brief minutes i.e. I cannot predict exactly as to time.
Pointing to each i.e. attributing to each minute (what will actually happen during it).
By oft predict By constantly saying (what I see in the stars).
I read such art i.e. I make my interpretations.
As truth and beauty ... If from thyself to store i.e. you would perpetuate your integrity and your beauty if you would turn away from self-sufficiency and get a son.
prognosticate Forecast.
date End.

Sonnet 15

Again the theme is the passing of time, with the imagery taking in the stage, the stars, plants all seen in relation to man (and, in the case of the friend, his beauty).

Holds in perfection Keeps in completeness.
That this huge stage The world compared to the theatre, as in 'All the world's a stage ...', the famous speech from *As You Like It*.

Whereon the stars in secret influence See the note on astrology in the previous sonnet, but note that the 'comment' here is silent.
Cheered and check'd even by the self-same sky At once encouraged and held back – a reference to the effect of Nature on the growth of plants; and to actors in the theatre (and life) being either acclaimed or booed.
Vaunt i.e. boast and brag.
at height decrease Fall from their prime.
brave state Showy self-display.
out of memory i.e. until they are forgotten (by those who saw them).
conceit of this inconstant stay i.e. the knowledge of change, of impermanence.
debateth Collaborates with decay.
And all in war with Time ... I engraft you new Out of love for you, I contend with time and fashion you, give you life, in my verse. The image is from the 'grafting' of trees.

Sonnet 16

The previous sonnet had the friend living in the poet's verse; this one suggests that he takes more practical means of perpetuating himself. Imagery of flowers and of drawing underlines the theme of the poem. The sonnet appears almost as an extension of the previous one, the first line referring back to the 'grafting'.

mightier i.e. by more practical means (sexual intercourse).
blessed ... barren The two words immediately contrast – the first indicates the coming child, the second the fact that verse begets nothing.
the top of happy hours i.e. in your prime.
maiden gardens ... unset Virgin soil . . . unsown with seed (the sexual connotation is at once obvious).
With virtuous wish i.e. would be gratified to bear.
painted counterfeit Picture (though whether in verse or a portrait painting is not clear).

the lines of life that life repair Heavy punning, since the reference is directly to children, but this brings to mind the lines in the forehead of age as well, and the pencil lines which add to the punning sequence. 'Repair' is 'renew' (through begetting a child).

Time's pencil Small paint-brush.

pupil pen i.e. serving, apprentice (note again the running alliteration here).

inward worth nor outward fair i.e. your integrity and character or your personal beauty.

Can make you live yourself i.e. keep you alive.

To give away yourself i.e. in the act of sexual intercourse or by giving yourself to someone – in marriage, for instance.

still Always.

And you must live, drawn i.e. procreate the living image of your own beauty.

Sonnet 17

Here the poet returns not merely to the contemplation of the friend, but to the contemplation of the effect his verse will have in recording that friend's superior qualities. He comes to the conclusion that his work will be criticized for its exaggeration or distortion, and this leads him happily to the succinct couplet that if his friend has a child he will live twice over – in the poet's verse and in the child he has sired.

Who will believe Note the directness of the opening, almost anticipating the metaphysical poems of John Donne ('Busy old fool . . .'; but earlier sonnets too struck sometimes a colloquial note, like Sidney's 'Dear, why make you more of a dog than me?').

a tomb i.e. a monument, which commemorates the dead.

your parts Both your physical beauty and your intellect.

fresh numbers Vivid poetry (compare Pope's assertion 'I lisped in numbers for the numbers came').

touches . . . touch'd The favourite device of repetition involving word-play.

yellow'd with their age Although he is speaking of his poems, the phrase is to be associated with the man who dies old and heirless.

your true rights i.e. what you deserve, the praise you should have received.

And stretched metre of an antique song This much-quoted line simply means 'the distortions present in a poetical mode which is now outdated'.

that time i.e. then, when the above was said.

Sonnet 18

This is one of the most celebrated of the sonnets, and its popularity can be easily understood. From the opening question we are carried along on a superb rhythmic fluency, with end-stopped lines not arresting the flow of the argument but rather making for definitive statements within it. The return is to the theme of immortality through verses, but takes in the impermanence of Nature.

a summer's day There is a strong suggestion that this really refers to the season of summer rather than an isolated day in it.

lovely Kind and good-natured.

temperate i.e. moderate, good-tempered.

darling Presumably a term of affection for the beauty of nature.

May In Elizabethan times this implied May–June.

lease ... date Note the use of the image, implying 'taken for a time'.

too hot ... dimm'd i.e. the contrasts in the weather (with the implication of the contrasts in life).

fair from fair ... chance ... untrimm'd The idea is that things change – human life changes and declines, even as Nature is stripped of her beauty.

lose possession ... ow'st i.e. the beauty you *own* will be perpetuated (in my verses).

When in eternal lines Enshrined in my verses, you will last for all time.

So long as men Note the simplicity, of structure and phrasing of this couplet on immortality.

Sonnet 19

An extension of the poet's perennial theme, but contrasting markedly with Sonnet 18's serenity in its violent associations and images – the idea being that Time can 'devour' anything in Nature but must spare 'my love's fair brow'. Yet in the end the poet reflects that this beauty will be preserved in his verses.

blunt thou the lion's paws i.e. as it gets older, it loses its power.
And make the earth devour her own sweet brood Everything returns to the earth – animals, plants, man, in the final instance. The line is about the inevitability of death.
burn the long-liv'd phoenix The legendary phoenix was known for its longevity as well as for the fact that it was consumed alive in its own 'blood' on its funeral pyre, and then rose renewed from the ashes. It was reputed to live for five or six centuries.
fleets Fleetest, i.e. pass.
carve not with thy hours i.e. do not put lines in.
thine antique pen Probably 'grotesque', because of the changes wrought in a person's appearance by the passage of time.
Him in thy course untainted i.e. let him remain unspoiled by your passage.
beauty's pattern i.e. as the type or symbol of beauty.
love . . . live The key words in the poem, and indeed in most of the sonnets.

Sonnet 20

One of the focal points of interpretation, because of the reference to the 'master-mistress' and the basic difficulties of identification behind the coinage. The friend's beauty is here compared to that of a woman, and he also has other virtues associated with women, as well as a man's 'hue'. The sestet marks something of a transition, since the poet develops the conceit that the friend was originally intended to be a woman, but turned out to be a man, with the result that the poet is cheated of his fulfilment. However, the poet can still love his friend, who for his part can also yield woman the 'treasure' of fulfilment.

master-mistress Written without the hyphen, this probably means 'pre-eminent', though Shakespeare may be mocking the mistress convention of his fellow sonneteers by praising a man: with the hyphen, it must mean 'man as mistress'.

passion Here we can run the gamut of association, from sexual passion on the one hand, through love, to the conventional expression of 'passion' in the form of this poem.

less false in rolling This implies that women are not to be trusted, are fickle and flirtatious.

Gilding the object i.e. adding to its value (the friend's eye being compared to the light of the sun).

hue all hues In appearance better (than all others).

Which steals i.e. the appearance.

amazeth Confuses.

And for a woman These lines seem to mean 'You were originally made as a woman, but Nature being over-fond of you as she made you, made you a man, thus depriving me of you'.

prick'd thee out i.e. selected you, made you for. The bawdy play on 'prick'd' will be obvious if the student looks back to the preceding lines, where the physical addition which made the friend a man is directly indicated.

thy love's use i.e. they are fortunate to have you use them (make physical love to them).

Sonnet 21

This sonnet has been something of a critical battleground, for a reason different from that of the previous one; since it refuses to employ extravagant conceits – which the previous sonnets do – Shakespeare's authorship has been called in question. To this writer it appears to be merely a change of mood for the word-play is still present, and there is a fine, balanced control throughout.

that Muse i.e. the other kind of poet. Some critics have thought that this condemnation of falseness is the first attack on the rival poet.
for ornament doth use i.e. draws his decorative imagery from.
And every fair ... rehearse i.e. compares his mistress with everything beautiful that occurs to him.
couplement of proud compare i.e. a heaping up of 'smug' comparisons.
That heaven's air in this huge rondure hems Hemmed in by the great roundness of the world.
gold candles i.e. the stars.
that like of hearsay well Those who live to repeat what they have picked up. The implication is that 'they' use second-hand conceits.
I will not The general meaning appears to be 'I will not prostitute myself by such false usage'.

Sonnet 22

The theme in the initial lines is of growing old, but this gives way to the poet's knowledge that the beauty of his friend lives in him also, and is an adornment to him. The final section is a word-playing confession of his love.

glass Mirror.
of one date i.e. last, exist together.
furrows Lines.
Then look I death ... expiate i.e. I look to death to make an end of me.
seemly raiment i.e. fitting garment.
chary Cautious(ly).
Presume not on ... to give back again These lines appear to mean that 'the friend must not think that he will be "heart-free" when the poet dies, since the latter possesses for ever his friend's heart'. This is difficult to render colloquially, since the word-play is tightly organized.

Sonnet 23

The analogy, as often with Shakespeare, is with the playhouse he knew so well. The comparison of the actor's fear or rage with the poet's own excess of emotion is sustained throughout the octave; the latter can express that love through his works, but not in the loved one's actual presence. Some editors prefer 'looks' to 'books' in line 9, but the arguments for 'books' seem to this editor to be unanswerable.

unperfect i.e. not word perfect.
replete . . . rage Overcome with his anger.
Whose strength's abundance i.e. so strong in his anger/emotion that he is unable to act.
for fear of trust i.e. having no faith in myself, lacking self-confidence.
The perfect ceremony of love's rite i.e. (forget to say) what is properly due to love – that is, I can't speak my love as I feel it should be spoken.
O'ercharg'd with burthen My feeling of love is so strong that it makes me inarticulate.
my books i.e. my poems – let them speak for me.
dumb presagers Silent speakers for me.
for recompense i.e. some return (of my love).
More than that tongue The play on 'more' runs through this line. The first mention obviously looks back to 'recompense', but the others refer to the fulsome praise of beauty.
To hear with eyes belongs to love's fine wit i.e. you have to be sensitive and perceptive to enable one sense to translate the effects of another.

Sonnet 24

This time the analogy is with art, though the rival claims of 'steel'd' and 'stell'd' have exercised the various interpreters. The conceit is elaborated throughout the octave, and continued into the sestet, but the couplet falls away somewhat, or perhaps takes a different direction from the customary one, for the implication is that painters draw only what they see, and cannot paint the inner man.

stell'd Engraved.
table Tablet. The picture would be engraved on this.
perspective From the correct focus or angle.
his windows i.e. those of his 'bosom's shop'.
Yet eyes this cunning want i.e. eyes lack the skill to complete what they see (they can't see the true man inside the body).

Sonnet 25

Another expression of love, the analogies ranging from those who are public figures to those who were famous in the past, the implication being that the poet in his love is more complete since it is returned and since he cannot be displaced from it.

in favour with their stars i.e. who enjoy good fortune. As we have seen, Shakespeare uses the image in earlier sonnets.
whom fortune of such triumph bars i.e. (I) am denied such pomp and acclaim.
Unlook'd for joy i.e. I delight in what was beyond my hope.
But as the marigold Only as the marigold does when the sun is out.
And in themselves their pride lies buried 'When it is dark their beauty is no longer seen', but there is the suggestion too that their showy appearance dies with them.
at a frown The analogy is with the 'princes' favourites', with here the suggestion of lost favour.
The painful warrior famoused for might i.e. the enduring soldier made famous by his strength.
once foil'd i.e. defeated.
rased i.e. erased, struck off. (Compare Ulysses in *Troilus and Cressida*, III.2.145: 'Time hath, my lord, a wallet at his back/Wherein he puts aims for oblivion'.)
Where I may not remove, nor be remov'd 'Where I cannot be displaced or be inconstant.' The first usage looks back to the 'princes' favourites'.

Sonnet 26

Extravagant language here, with the idea of the vassal sending the poem to his feudal lord as a verbal 'ambassage'. This is connected to the thought that the lord will 'clothe' his ideas with kindness, so that good fortune will bless him. Then he will be put to the test.

vassalage i.e. in feudal service.
Thy merit hath i.e. I am bound to you through your superior qualities.
ambassage i.e. embassy, message.
To witness duty . . . wit i.e. to bear witness to my duty, not to show off my literary ability.
wit Further word-play, here meaning 'intelligence'.
good conceit Bright idea.
In thy soul's thought, all naked, will bestow it i.e. that you will give some hospitality or accommodation to this 'naked' expression of my duty.
that guides my moving Probably, quite simply, watches over my life's journey.
Points on me i.e. shines.
fair aspect Favourable sign.
And puts apparel i.e. 'clothes my tattered expression of love'.
To show me worthy To present me as being worthy of my beloved (the reference is to his duty and his wit).
prove me i.e. test me out.

Sonnet 27

This describes the torture of love, for the body tired with the day's work can find no rest because of thoughts of the beloved and the working of the imagination. As always the imagery is cleverly balanced, the day's journey being contrasted with the journey of thought. The language is less elevated than in some of the earlier poems, but there is one exquisite line: 'Looking on darkness which the blind do see'.

travel Probably a pun on 'travail' (labour) too.
Intend Set out (links with 'pilgrimage.).
Looking ... see i.e. looking on that darkness which the blind see permanently.
imaginary sight i.e. the eye of the imagination.
their shadow Their representation of you ('their' being the poet's thoughts).
her old face new Night is seen as something fearful ('ghastly') and therefore she is 'old' rather than young like the friend. Juliet was such a jewel upon the cheek of night.
quiet Peace, tranquillity.

Sonnet 28

This sonnet obviously follows on from the last, with much play on the balancing of day and night. This continues into the sestet in the paired-off images before the couplet, when both are bound together again in contrast with the telling technical achievement of the longer last line, which reflects the length of the night.

plight Condition or state.
debarr'd Denied.
either's i.e. to each other's (reign). Night and day are seen as in natural opposition.
in consent i.e. by agreement.
The one by toil i.e. the day's work.
to complain i.e. causing me to complain.
the day, to please him Elliptical construction – 'in order to please him'.
thou art bright i.e. the friend.
dost him grace i.e. do him proud, bless him (by your presence).
flatter ... swart-complexion'd Deceive ... black-coloured.
twire Peep.
gild'st i.e. you make the night beautiful by your presence.
But day doth daily ... length seem stronger A fine couplet, the structure of which echoes the length of suffering – 'Each day my sorrows increase in length, and each night my sorrows likewise increase in strength.'

Sonnet 29

This captures the mood of depression, the moment that comes to all of us when we feel low, the momentary jealousy and envy we sometimes feel. But, in the sestet, the mood changes – to the harmony of remembered love. This is a popular sonnet, because, the language is simple and direct (despite archaisms like 'bootless') and also because it is a resolution of negative emotions that we know only too well. It is a fine evocation of mood, of mercurial human nature.

in disgrace with Fortune i.e. not favoured, when things are not going well (for me).

outcast state i.e. lonely situation. Note the way in which 'state' is a key word here, since it will recur with so different an emphasis in the last line.

bootless Unavailing.

Featur'd like him, like him The poet is now moving from person to person, envying particular qualities or talents in each.

art Skill, ability.

scope This word implies 'width' of ability in which to achieve something.

With what I most enjoy Perhaps 'I am not contented with what I can do, because it is so limited'.

Haply By chance.

sullen earth It appears to be sullen because it has not yet shaken off night.

Sonnet 30

This is similar in tone to the previous poem, with a gliding alliterative effect in the first line and correspondingly heavier sequences later in the poem. The personal note as distinct from the poetic exercise is very strong indeed, and again the poem is expressive of the power that memory has over us all.

When to the sessions i.e. when I think about (what has happened in the past). It has been noted that the language of this sonnet (sessions . . . account . . . pay) is the language of a court; it is almost as if the poet is conducting his own 'sessions' and giving some kind of judgement between past and present.

the lack i.e. the fact that I didn't achieve what I wished.

And with old woes new wail my dear times waste A complex line which appears to mean, 'My old disappointments return as if fresh, and I am made miserable again by thinking of them'. Thus they cost him 'dear'.

drown an eye i.e. weep copiously.

dateless night i.e. the eternal darkness of death.

And weep afresh Cry again over the misery of a love long since over and gone.

expense Loss.

foregone Over, finished with.

heavily . . . tell o'er Miserably count my sufferings (of the past).

fore-bemoaned moan i.e. which I complained about in the past.

All losses are restor'd Again the legal hint in the language – I get back all that I lost (merely by thinking of you).

Sonnet 31

Again a continuation of the conceit in the previous sonnet, but with a subtle turn which states that all those beloved of the poet in the past – all the friends now dead – really live on in the beautiful form and person of this friend. The sonnet is characterized by imagery of the grave and of religious love.

endeared with all hearts i.e. made more loving by embodying others.

by lacking Because I lost them.

all love's loving parts All aspects of the poet's love for his friends (are present in this friend).

obsequious Deeply reverent.

dear religious love i.e. devout, deeply felt.

As interest of the dead i.e. what is due to the dead, the claim they make upon me.

which now appear Who now are seen as.

remov'd This has the sense of being moved not to the grave but to the friend.

Thou art the grave A favourite Shakespearean image.

trophies i.e. memorials. The idea is that they are 'memories' which the poet finds by contemplating his beloved friend.

all their parts See note above on line 3 of this sonnet.

That due of many i.e. what I owed my friends I now owe to you.

all they, hast all the all of me Fine word-play, meaning 'since all of them are now in you, and I love you, they have all my love'.

Sonnet 32

The theme is again the idea of death and the poet's survival in the lines he has written to his friend. There is a strong awareness of the literary achievement of others and perhaps some of the self-doubt of the true artist. He visualizes his death occurring before that of his (younger) friend, and asks the latter to value him for his love, rather than for his inferior verse.

my well-contented day Somewhat paradoxical. It appears to mean (in view of the next line), 'the day I die, which I shall welcome'.

churl Death Personification, with Death doing the burying in a rough uncouth way.

rude lines i.e. roughly constructed.

the bettering of the time i.e. those who write better.

Reserve them i.e. keep them.

Exceeded by the height of happier men i.e. surpassed by the elevated poetry of those who were happier than myself.

Muse grown with this growing age i.e. (had my friend's) poetic talent kept pace with these fine literary times.

in ranks of better equipage i.e. with poets of splendid literary worth.

poets better prove i.e. are better than he was. (Could it be that Shakespeare is being ironic?)
his for his love i.e. his sincerity.

Sonnet 33

Another of the more celebrated sonnets, though it has caused considerable critical dissension. The broad comparison is of the separation, the sun effaced by clouds. The note of unhappiness in love, of estrangement from the beloved, is now being sounded.

Flatter ... sovereign Despite the natural description, these words are suggestive also of Court and the favours of a monarch. 'Flatter' really means 'irradiate' here.
alchemy Transmutation into gold: the sun is heaven's alchemist.
Anon After a time.
basest Lowest, most disreputable.
ugly rack This is a reference to the effect of the clouds: the drifting clouds disfigure the 'celestial face'.
forlorn world i.e. made forlorn by the loss of the brightness.
Stealing unseen i.e. moving away furtively.
my sun i.e. the friend.
But out alack But alas he was mine for so short a time.
region cloud The aerial cloud. (The meaning is that he is hidden by cloud: something has come between them.)
Yet him for this Yet despite this my love for him has not decreased one jot.
stain ... staineth Grow pale, lose their radiance.

Sonnet 34

This is in the same vein as the previous poem, but is certainly less stately. Since the address is directly to the beloved, the tone is more conversational. The dual imagery is of Nature and of injury. The central analogy is the sun/friend, with the quality of the day reflecting the nature of their relationship.

thy bravery The beneficence (of the sun), or the amiability (of the friend).

rotten smoke i.e. foul, disgusting exhalations (there may also be a reference to deceit).

cures not the disgrace i.e. does not alter the fact that there is a scar.

thy shame give physic to my grief Nor can your sense of shame assuage my suffering.

I have still the loss i.e. I have the sense of losing you.

weak relief Feeble compensation.

bears ... cross i.e. suffers. (Could there be a reference to the Crucifixion? The original has 'loss'.)

those tears are pearl which thy love sheds i.e. the tears you weep from regret are precious to me.

ransom all ill deeds i.e. compensate for the actions (which have hurt me).

Sonnet 35

Again the analogy with Nature is pressed, but this gives place to self-examination, to considerable word-play extending into the sestet, and before the concluding couplet, to legal and war images.

stain i.e. overcome, dim.

canker This is a larva which eats away the bud from inside. It occurs also in the plays, where (following biblical usage) it means, too, a sore or ulcer, also the dog-rose.

make faults i.e. are guilty of error.

Authorizing thy trespass with compare Justifying your fault by comparison with my own.

Myself corrupting, salving thy amiss By palliating your guilt I make myself guilty.

Excusing thy sins more than their sins are Probably this is a reference to the 'natural' sinners (roses and fountains, for example) who have no moral sense of sin and are therefore excused by the poet.

thy sensual fault ... sense (I) bring reason, balance to any fault of the flesh; any self-indulgence has my sympathy.

adverse ... advocate A play on words – he who should be against you is for you.
lawful plea Again the 'legal' language employed in a reasoned prosecution of his own error.
civil war i.e. conflict within me.
accessary i.e. accessory, helper, pleader for.
To that sweet thief ... me i.e. I support you, whom I love, though you hurtfully deprive me of yourself.

Sonnet 36

This sonnet deals with separation in love in order to preserve the reputation of the beloved; it is a poem of self-denial. Again there is a directness about the conversational tone, an acceptance of the inevitable rather than sublimation.

Let me confess I have to admit that.
our undivided loves i.e. although our love is not separated – we love one another – we must be separated physically.
those blots Either stains – on the character, or moral blemishes, or some form of disgrace.
one respect One certainty.
a separable spite i.e. (we are) divided by fate, which harms us.
alter not love's sole effect i.e. does not change the unifying fact of our love.
not evermore Never again.
my bewailed guilt i.e. my anguished self-confession.
in such sort In such a way.
mine is thy good report My love for you makes me identify with you so completely that I feel your 'good name' becomes also mine.

Sonnet 37

This sonnet has proved a hunting-ground for biographical interpretations, most of them surrounding the word 'lame' in its literal sense. To some extent, it echoes 'When in disgrace with fortune and men's eyes', with the poet regarding himself as being in adversity, but taking comfort from the fact of his love and 'That I in thy abundance am suffic'd'.

made lame by Fortune's dearest spite i.e. injured by the grievous malice of fate. No physical injury is implied here.
my comfort of thy worth and truth i.e. I console myself with your sincerity and integrity.
Entitled in their parts do crowned sit i.e. are the natural aristocracy, and thus rule.
I make my love engrafted to this store I graft my love on to these qualities (beauty, birth, wealth, wit).
shadow . . . substance The contrast which has been previously used – the image of the beloved endows the poet with something of his qualities.
suffic'd i.e. rewarded, satisfied.
Look what Whatever.

Sonnet 38

A sonnet in praise of the inspiration which the friend provides to the poet. Again the literary awareness and ambition are present.

want subject to invent i.e. lack ideas – (how can I) be at loss for something to write?
Thine own sweet argument *You* are my theme.
For every vulgar paper to rehearse (You are too good) to be the subject of common hacks.
aught Anything.
stands against thy sight i.e. comes to your attention.
gives invention light i.e. provide inspiration.
the tenth Muse There were nine Muses, the daughters of Zeus and Mnemosyne. The term 'tenth Muse' has been applied to various admired writers.
invocate i.e. invoke, call to their aid.
Eternal numbers 'Numbers' here means 'verses'. Verses that will outlast Time.

my slight Muse Either modesty or irony sired this phrase.
curious days i.e. very critical, weighing things minutely.
pain Care, trouble.

Sonnet 39

There is considerable play in this poet with the idea that in praising his beloved he is in fact praising himself, since the friend is 'the better part of me'. The fact that they live separate lives means that the poet can praise his friends the more, absence being filled with thoughts of love. ('Absence makes the heart grow fonder'.)

with manners i.e. with propriety, with becoming modesty.
What can mine own praise ... when I praise thee Typical Shakespearean play on words, roughly meaning 'What can I gain from praising myself? And yet when I praise you I am really praising myself.' This makes obvious sense if it is seen in relation to line 2.
Even for this i.e. in view of this, because of this.
dear love Precious.
lose name of single one i.e. yield the reputation of being united.
That due to thee i.e. accord you your deserved praise or honour.
To entertain the time i.e. spend it pleasantly.
Which time and thoughts so sweetly dost deceive The subject appears to be 'love' which 'dost deceive' – perhaps because it makes dreams or illusions.
And that thou teachest ... hence remain The difficulty of interpretation lies in the construction; the lines seem to mean that one person is made into two; (i) by being absent; (ii) by being present in the poet's 'lines' – the whole of the sonnet.

Sonnet 40

Word-play throughout, notably on the word 'love' which makes interpretation difficult: repetitive, antithetical, paradoxical, with mixed imagery, this appears to be an inventive exercise that moves from the demands of the word-play to a plea to his friend for moderation and tolerance.

Take all my loves i.e. everything I love.
What hast thou then What have you gained from all this?
true love call i.e. constancy.
All mine was thine ... hadst this more You had all my love anyway (before I made the declaration) (in line 1).
my love receivest (My mistress.) The play on 'love' means that it is infinitely ambiguous in this sonnet, and quite deliberately so. It is an exercise in ingenuity and word-play.
for my love thou usest The obvious meaning is sexual – you are free to 'use' my mistress.
wilful taste i.e. sexual liking for.
all my poverty i.e. my small means.
To bear love's wrong than hate's known injury (We suffer more) if we are betrayed in love than if we experience someone's hate.
Lascivious grace (This is an 'oxymoron', a figure of speech containing seeming contradictions.) The meaning here is lustful honour or beneficence.
spites i.e. injuries (of a moral or emotional nature).

Sonnet 41

The love poetry here takes the form of an analysis of temptation and its effect on the poet, on the beloved, and on their affairs, however casual or unimportant. The first section considers all the temptations the beloved has in himself and those which may assail him; but the sestet implies a relationship between the poet's mistress and the friend. The tone is somewhat different here, but the couplet succinctly defines the sin.

pretty wrongs that liberty commits i.e. venial sins emanating from licentiousness; sexual freedom.
full well befits It is to be expected (in view of your attractions).

still Always.
Gentle thou art You are easy-going, and therefore you are vulnerable to persuasion.
therefore to be assailed i.e. you are open to seduction.
sourly leave her ... have prevailed Boorishly go . . . until he has had his way (sexually).
thou might'st my seat forbear i.e. leave my mistress alone.
chide ... straying youth Curb your lawless desires.
riot i.e. indulgence of lust.
a twofold truth Probably 'troth', so that there is a double deception.
Hers ... Thine Note the antithesis of the couplet.

Sonnet 42

The theme of the friend enjoying the poet's mistress is further explored here: in the first part of the octave the poet bewails the loss of his friend rather than that of his mistress; but the mood changes in the second part here to one of forgiveness rather than lamentation. By the couplet the poet has so turned about his own arguments that 'my friend and I are one'.

it is not all my grief i.e. that is not its sum total.
That she ... my wailing chief i.e. that *she* possesses *you* is my greatest complaint.
Loving offenders i.e. the friend and the mistress.
I will excuse ye I will make excuses for you.
Suff'ring my friend for my sake to approve her i.e. letting my friend test her (sexually) *and* form a good opinion of her.
my love's gain My mistress's enjoyment.
losing her Note the repetition of the word in one form or another, and the way 'loss' and 'gain' are balanced in this poem.
I lose both twain i.e. I lose friend and mistress.
lay on me this cross i.e. this burden of suffering.
my friend and I are one The idea is of being made 'one' by love, and this explains the last line, the poet stating that 'she loves but me alone', since he *is* as one person with his friend.

Sonnet 43

This marks a return to an earlier theme, though it is rather differently developed here, with his friends' absence affecting his sleep and dreams; there is a marked juggling with light and dark, which are seen as the contrasts of presence and absence and the allied alternations of mood.

When most I wink When my eyes are closed.
unrespected i.e. without noticing.
And darkly bright, are bright in dark directed Note the alliterative force as well as the word-play – the meaning appears to be that 'my eyes see bright and clearly in the darkness though they are closed'.
shadow Image.
shadows The darkness itself. Note the contrast.
How would thy shadow's form form happy show How would your body itself add radiance.
shade See note p.44.
imperfect shade i.e. nebulous image.
on sightless eyes doth stay i.e. this image remains with me though my eyes are closed in sleep (or perhaps even feigned sleep).
All days are nights to see i.e. each day has the appearance of darkness (until I see you).
when dreams do show thee me i.e. as the popular song has it, 'I'll see you in my dreams'.

Sonnet 44

This shows a slight variation in the rhyme-scheme, whereby the 'a' rhyme is employed again in the sestet. Thus it is ababcdcdaeaeff. The theme is again absence, with the play on the idea of flesh being thought, and thus inseparable from the beloved. In the second part of the octave this is explored through 'nimble thought', but the penalties of its not being 'pure' thought lead to the frustrations of the sestet.

dull substance i.e. my heavy body.

Injurious distance i.e. separation which does us injury, or cruelty.

limits Places

although my foot did stand i.e. if I was (far from you).

As soon as think the place where he would be i.e. thought can be at once wherever he (= it) wishes.

thought kills me that I am not thought i.e. I am desolate, knowing that I am not completely thought. (As T. S. Eliot puts it, 'Between the idea/And the reality . . . Falls the Shadow.')

so much of earth and water wrought i.e. I am made of my heavy body as well as my emotions, my tears.

Receiving naught . . . either's woe The couplet is a complex one. It seems to mean that being chained to the body and its limitations, the poet gains only suffering – the inability to be where his friend is, and the tears which attend his frustration.

Sonnet 45

This appears to be a straightforward sequel to the previous Sonnet, for the poet picks up where he left off by referring to the other two elements – air and fire – after his use of earth and water in the preceding poem. By the second half of the octave these elements – which here represent thought and desire – have gone to the beloved, leaving the poet weighed down with melancholy. When they return he is filled with joy, only to be depressed again when he once more sends them forth.

slight air and purging fire i.e. having little substance (air), but having purifying qualities (fire).

abide Am, may be.

The first my thought In this poem air is equated with thought and fire with desire for the beloved.

present-absent The term implies change, or perhaps that the elements are at one time with the poet, then absent from him.

quicker elements i.e. more vital forces.

tender embassy i.e. loving journey (to you).

being made of four See Sonnet 44. The reference is to the four elements.

melancholy This was a 'humour', cold and dry. Here it is associated with miserable, abject heaviness of spirit.

life's composition be recured Probably 'until I am restored to balance or even health'.

those swift messengers i.e. thought and desire.

even but now At this time.

assured ... recounting (When they return) they assure me of (your good health).

no longer glad i.e. because the loved one – the friend – is still absent from him.

Sonnet 46

Shakespeare here develops the conceit of a dispute between the eye and the heart over precedence in love; and there is parallel legal imagery. Basically, the theme is that the heart is the storehouse of love, but it is the eye that sees the beauty of the beloved. The sestet contains a variant, since the last three lines have the same rhyme: ababcdcdefefff.

the conquest The idea seems to be that of 'sharing out the virtues' of the beloved.

Mine eye my heart thy picture's sight would bar My eye would wish to prevent my heart from seeing you (or a picture of you).

My heart mine eye the freedom of that right My heart would wish to prevent my eye from having the right to see you.

A closet Small room, locked case.

crystal i.e. clear (a favourite Elizabethan usage).

the defendant Legal image – linked with 'plea' – and the reference here is to the eyes.

in him thy fair appearance lies i.e. the eyes have the reflection of the beloved (and hence have the right to possess him or his portrait).

To 'cide this title is impanelled A difficult line. 'To decide which has precedence a jury of thoughts is summoned' (see next line in the sonnet).

eyes moiety ... heart's part i.e. what share or portion belonged to the eyes and the heart.

mine eye's due . . . heart The couplet gives a predictable, balanced judgement: the eye has what it sees, the heart has what is unseeable – love.

Sonnet 47

This follows on from the previous sonnet, with the heart and eye, at first 'at a mortal war' then finally in conjunction or alliance. That these two sonnets are about a portrait of the beloved is clear from lines 5–6 here: the war is over, and both heart and eyes gain from their loving interaction, with the couplet cleverly rounding off their 'league' in dreams.

a league is took i.e. an alliance set up.
famish'd for a look i.e. longing for sight of the beloved.
feast . . . painted banquet Note that this connected image implies appetite, strength of feeling, conjured up by the picture.
are present still with me i.e. although you are absent, because of your division between sharing my heart and eyes, you are always with me.
no farther than my thoughts i.e. you cannot move outside the range of my thinking.
thy picture in my sight i.e. the portrait I have of you in my imagination.

Sonnet 48

The elaborate working out of a conceit which considers that material possessions are locked away lest they be stolen, but the poet has let his beloved be 'the prey of every vulgar thief', and fears that, though his love is enclosed in his breast, it too will be stolen away. The tone is conversational, the language not sufficiently raised to make this more than a clever exercise on the theme indicated above.

when I took my way Presumably, when I had gone away.
truest bars i.e. strong security.
to my use it might unused stay Literally, it might not be available until I needed it – in other words, that it might be safe, protected from those who would take it.

Thou best of dearest, and mine only care You, most precious to me and my chief concern in life.
Art left the prey Because all can see you, and thus steal your looks and treasure them.
in any chest Note the pun – a treasure-chest, and the chest of the poet which contains another treasure – his heart.
thou art not, though I feel thou art The movement of this sentence is expressive of doubt.
come and part i.e. enter and leave (at your will).
For truth proves thievish for a prize so dear The implication is that honesty or integrity will not be able to resist the temptation of the friend's beauty.

Sonnet 49

The interesting innovation in this poem is the repetition of 'Against that time' with its look into the future and its appraisal of the nature of rejection; the poem has a realistic element and not a merely cynical one, since it accepts that time changes feelings, and that expediency can make a mockery of the past. The effect of the repetition is to give an insistence, a reality to what is to come, as distinct from the present enjoyment of favour.

Against that time i.e. To prepare for the eventuality.
hath cast his utmost sum Has drawn up his final account.
Call'd to that audit by advis'd respects i.e. required to render account based on the careful weighing of the facts (of our love).
strangely pass i.e. when you pass me as a stranger would.
converted Changed or transformed is probably the best equivalent here.
Shall reasons find of settled gravity i.e. will discover reasons of unchanging seriousness.
ensconce Establish (myself), settle in snugly.
uprear/To guard the lawful reasons on thy part I raise my hand in front of me to protect myself against your justifiable argument.

the strength of laws i.e. of nature. But notice that the legal references underline the 'coldness' of what he fears will one day come.

Sonnet 50

This describes a journey away from his friend, and the suffering that he – and the beast who carries him – endures. It is conversational and undistinguished in tone, but reveals compassion – and self-pity!

How heavy i.e. miserable.
that ease and that repose i.e. comfort and peace or rest.
Thus far the miles i.e. every step I take is *away* from my friend.
tired with my woe Tired because I express my grief (by hitting him).
dully i.e. heavily – in mood approximating to that of his rider.
the wretch i.e. the horse.
lov'd not speed, being made from thee (As if he sensed) that his rider did not enjoy going quickly – at speed – from his beloved.
More sharp to me i.e. because it echoes the poet's mood, and also perhaps because he feels guilt at unnecessary spurring of the horse.
My grief lies onward As indeed does the horse's, if he is to be spurred!

Sonnet 51

A development of the previous poem; the argument is that there is no haste until the necessity arises – that is when he returns to his love. He concludes that no horse will then be able to keep up with his thoughts and emotions; but out of his love he will forgive the beast's tardiness.

slow offence i.e. the horse's fault in being so slow.

From where thou art . . . thence Why should I hurry away from where you are?

posting i.e. moving with great speed.

swift extremity Great haste.

Then should I spur . . . wind The image of riding the wind – or even the whirlwind – is a common one.

no motion shall I know I shan't be aware that I am moving.

of perfect'st love being made i.e. originating from complete love.

neigh Horse's neigh as mating sign, hence again comparing his return to his love to the impatience of his desire. (Compare *Venus and Adonis*, line 307, when Adonis's steed forsakes him, to pursue a mare: 'He looks upon his love, and neighs to her;').

But love, for love i.e. Love itself, in its generosity.

jade horse.

Since from thee . . . leave to go i.e. Since he went slowly when we left you, I'll run towards you myself and let him go on his own.

Sonnet 52

A finely balanced sonnet, which works through a number of connected images – treasure, jewellery, chest, for example – the number of images approximating to the variety of pleasure and hope which the poet has in the contemplation of his beloved, whether from near or far.

So am I as the rich I am just like the rich man.

sweet up-locked i.e. the locked-up treasure in which he delights.

he will not every hour i.e. he will not wish to see it all the time.

For blunting the fine point of seldom pleasure i.e. for fear of satiety.

so solemn and so rare i.e. formal and occasional.

set Placed.

captain jewels in the carcanet i.e. the most important stones in the necklace. This was often of gold, inlaid with gems.

as my chest i.e. retains you in a chest.

some special instant special blest The word-play really means a great moment in someone's life (involving the wearing of something splendid), as a wedding or even, perhaps, a royal occasion.

new unfolding his imprison'd pride i.e. revealing the quality of what lies within (the wardrobe).

Blessed are you ... to hope This couplet means that the friend is twice blessed: if he is present, the occasion is 'joyful' (triumph); if he is not, the poet still has the pleasure of hoping to see him in the future.

Sonnet 53

This takes as its central 'conceit' the friend's superiority to all those others, who are much praised – and indeed to all things in nature as well. This is further extended to imply that Nature itself partakes of the perfection of the friend, who is also the model of constancy.

substance Essential being.

strange shadows Not your own images but those of others wait on you.

Since every one hath Each person has his own shadow.

can every shadow lend This appears to mean that all that is beautiful, whatever type of beauty, can be supplied by you.

Adonis In legend, the beautiful youth beloved by Aphrodite.

counterfeit Picture.

Helen's cheek The legendary beauty married to Menelaus but carried off to Troy by the Trojan prince Paris, thus provoking the Greeks' ten years' siege of Troy.

tires i.e. robes or headgear.

spring ... foison This contrasts vernal freshness with the harvest.

shadow ... bounty The equivalent contrast to the above, with the implication that Nature is not as vital or as rich in produce as is the beauty of the friend.

in every blessed shape Nature but echoes you, or partakes of you.

But you like ... constant heart You are unique in your constancy.

Sonnet 54

Using the symbol of the rose, the poet here defines outward beauty and the beauty 'which truth doth give'. The canker parallel of an earlier sonnet is again used, the first two lines of the poem being the general statement; the next ten the rose analogy; while the couplet (with a problematical *by* or *my* reading) focuses on the friend and the perpetuation of his beauty.

sweet ornament which truth doth give i.e. by the gracious possession of integrity.
we it deem i.e. we believe it to be.
The canker blooms i.e. the flowers of the dog-rose. (See note on Sonnet 35.)
full as deep a dye As rich in colour as.
perfumed tincture Sweet-smelling colour.
masked buds discloses i.e. reveals their hidden buds.
their virtue only is their show i.e. their only beauty is their outward show.
unrespected Unnoticed.
Die to themselves Here again we are touching upon the earlier theme – nothing is influenced by their death.
sweet deaths ... sweetest odours i.e. perfumes.
that shall vade i.e. when your beauty has vanished, when you are old.
by (my) verse distils your truth Editors vary in their choice here: obviously 'your "truth" will survive in verse' is the main meaning.

Sonnet 55

One of the most celebrated of the sonnets, the tone here is measured and stately throughout; it is a proclamation of immortality through verse. The passage of time is depicted chiefly through the ravages of war; and the underlying theme is that the word lives longer than the sword, and art derides death.

Marble ... gilded monuments i.e. statues or monuments raised by rulers.
powerful rhyme Note how quickly the word echoes back to the descriptions of temporal power we have just seen. Shakespeare may simply be claiming that verse itself is powerful.
in these contents My poems.
unswept stone i.e. a neglected grave or monument, which has been left at the mercy of the weather.
wasteful war i.e. which destroys (what man has made).
broils Tumults.
work of masonry i.e. the mason's skill.
The living record i.e. the poet's verses.
all oblivious enmity The hostility which, careless of what it does, destroys all.
pace forth i.e. fearlessly.
still find room Will always be seen.
That wear this world out to the ending doom That succeed each other while man endures.
the judgement i.e. the final judgement (the 'ending doom').
dwell in lovers' eyes i.e. because, being lovers they partake of your beauty by themselves being in love.

Sonnet 56

There is almost a duality of theme here, since the poet is pleading for a renewal of the power of love – he appears to have fallen into an abject state – but at the same time one feels that this apathy may have been brought about by absence. The sonnet also records in the second part of the octave that change of mood common to lovers; and looks forward to the sestet in which the temporary nature of the feeling is compared to the necessity of enduring winter in order fully to enjoy the summer.

Sweet Love i.e. the emotion of love.
by feeding is allay'd i.e. desire is fulfilled, satisfied.
Tomorrow sharpen'd i.e. love is ever renewed.
they wink with fulness i.e. close because they are satiated.
see again i.e. come alive.
sad interim i.e. this sorrowful period.
Which parts the shore ... view The picture in these lines is of lovers separated by a stretch of water; the two have recently become engaged, and come each day to the shore in order to look across and see each other. ('return of love' means that their love is sustained, 'renewed' by the sight of each other.)
As call it winter ... rare The couplet seems to mean 'Just as winter, being so mournful, makes the summer more grateful since we have wished for it so strongly.'

Sonnet 57

The theme of this popular sonnet is that of slavery in love, and yet the nature of love demands such a complete giving up to the 'sovereign'. There is a crispness of utterance here that shows favourably against the extravagant word-play of the previous sonnets.

but tend ... desire i.e. wait upon you.
till you require i.e. until you want me.
chide the world-without-end-hour i.e. curse the length of time.
servant i.e. slave to your wants, not merely in the sense of attendant but also in the sense of lover.
or your affairs suppose i.e. guess at what you are doing.
So true a fool is love ... he thinks no ill i.e. love is so real and constant that whatever is done by the beloved is accepted.

Sonnet 58

A reworking, with variations, of the previous conceit; the first three lines indicate the poet's belief that he should in no way interfere with or comment upon the way his friend spends his time, but there is irony in the fourth line. The next four lines appear to exploit his suffering, and this runs into the sestet with an assertion that for what the friend does he alone is answerable. The couplet concludes this suffering-in-silence.

in thought control your times of pleasure i.e. exert an influence on you when you were enjoying yourself.

the account of hours to crave i.e. (that I should demand) to know how you have spent your time.

Being your vassal bound . . . leisure As I am your slave, I have to wait until you choose to tell me something.

beck Nod.

The imprison'd absence of your liberty The poet is separated from his friend, who has the freedom to do what he wishes. Such separation is equivalent in the poet's eyes to imprisonment.

And patience-tame, to sufferance bide each check It appears to mean '(I must) make myself tamely patient and endure all suffering (without ever accusing you of doing an injustice).'

list Please i.e. be where you wish to be.

charter i.e. privilege, and the power it involves.

privilege your time i.e. enjoy yourself as you think fit.

Yourself to pardon of self-doing crime You alone can forgive any sin against your own better nature.

Not blame your pleasure i.e. not to find fault with your enjoyment.

Sonnet 59

This sonnet is built around the idea – derived basically from the Pythagorean and Stoic philosophy – that there are cycles of life which are repeated, that there is nothing new but merely a repetition of former times and lives. Hence the starting-point of the conceit, and the poet's elaboration of it to fit his own particular case. There is also the astronomical belief that five hundred years would suffice for the world to re-enter a previous cycle; hence the possible reference in line 6 of this sonnet.

If there be nothing new And there is nothing new under the sun, a direct reference to *Ecclesiastes* 1, 9–10.
beguil'd i.e. deceived.
labouring for invention i.e. striving to find out.
bear amiss i.e. wrongly, mistakenly.
The second burthen of a former child Ironically, what has already been produced before.
Even of five hundred courses of the sun i.e. which would take one back into another cycle.
antique See note p.29.
Since mind at first in character was done From the time that man first set forth his views in writing.
composed wonder of your frame Your beautifully proportioned body.
Whether we are mended . . . they Whether we are an improvement, or whether they were better than we are.
revolution be the same i.e. when the cycle recurs are we exactly the same (as we were in that past existence)?
the wits The best brains.
To subjects worse i.e. this idea (but he may be laughing at himself for writing a poem about it!).

Sonnet 60

A fine sonnet on the theme of the changes wrought by time. Apart from its insight and its natural description, the poem has a kind of rhetorical flourish. Again the conclusion – but here it is modestly expressed – is that the poet's verse will live on despite the 'cruel hand' of time.

Like as i.e. just as.
pebbled shore The image suggests insecurity, movement with the pressure of the tide, and hence being subject to the cycles of time. (Compare Arnold's use of this powerful image in *Dover Beach*.)
In sequent toil all forwards do contend i.e. everything struggles forward, in due succession.
Nativity i.e. the newly born child.

the main of light i.e. an expanse of light; the sun, the day.
Crawls to maturity ... crown'd The line traces the child through life, and the sun to its zenith.
Crook'd eclipses ... fight Evil threatens his radiance, power. (In many mythologies heroes are pursued constantly by monsters, who at eclipses momentarily devour them.)
confound i.e. take away, destroy.
Time doth transfix the flourish set on youth i.e. the passing of time removes physical beauty.
delves the parallels ... brow Deepens the lines in the brow.
Feeds on the rarities of nature's truth (Time) takes away the finest and most perfect things in life.
And yet to times in hope my verse shall stand And yet I pray that in the future my poems will survive.
his cruel hand i.e. that of Time, personified throughout.

Sonnet 61

The basic theme in the first four lines is one of sleeplessness because of the intruding image of the beloved; in the second part of this octave the poet speculates on whether his friend's spirit visits him in order to find out how he has been passing his time. The sestet comes to the perhaps mundane conclusion that it is the poet's love that is responsible for his sleeplessness.

thy image i.e. the picture in my mind's eye.
shadows See note p.48.
thy spirit i.e. your essence.
shames and idle hours in me i.e. deeds which shame me, and idleness.
The scope and tenour ... jealousy i.e. the range of your jealous thoughts, and their direction.
From me far off, with others all too near The final line is implicit with jealousy – thus extending the reference in line 8 – for although it may be that the 'others all too near' refers to innocent friends, it could be that the reference is to the beloved's self-indulgence – i.e. with women.

Sonnet 62

This is a 'conceit' on the lover's self-identification with the beloved. In the first quatrain, he accuses himself of the 'sin of self-love'. The second finds the poet considering his own superiority to all others. The sestet opens with a contemplation of himself in the mirror, which shows the poet a self 'Beated and chopp'd with tann'd antiquity' – a self that could not possibly be the object of his love. The couplet confirms that all his praise has really been for the beloved, his other 'self', who has brought beauty into the ageing poet's life.

Sin of self-love Egoism, and conceit.
grounded inward i.e. deeply ingrained.
gracious i.e. full of grace.
No shape so true, no truth of such account 'I am perfectly proportioned, and this perfection is greatly to be admired'. (But the idea throughout is that the poet is not speaking of himself but of his friend; hence the friend's perfection here is being described).
And for myself . . . in all worths surmount For my own satisfaction I define my 'self' (the beloved) as being better than all others in every respect.
Beated and chopp'd with tann'd antiquity i.e. beaten (hence weatherbeaten) and chapped with age.
Self so self-loving were iniquity i.e. (having looked at myself in the mirror) it would be repugnant to love *that* self.
(my self) The beloved.
Painting my age with beauty of thy days Your youthful beauty embellishes my ageing appearance.

Sonnet 63

The return to a familiar theme, with a mixture of realistic and merely conventional treatment: that theme is the effects of age in the beloved, and the knowledge that he will live 'still green' in the 'black lines' of the poet, which will preserve forever the youth his friend has lost.

Against (When the time comes that.)

With Time's injurious hand crush'd and o'erworn It has been suggested here that the comparison is with clothes of which the nap is worn. Certainly the poet feels 'injuriously' (badly) used by Time.

hours have drained his blood i.e. he has been exhausted by life.

travail'd Punning effect here, of toil and of the journey through life – the combination of both.

steepy night Refers back to 'youthful morn', another analogy between the sun (youth) and night (old age).

Stealing away i.e. pilfering.

his spring i.e. his youthfulness.

For such a time i.e. when he (the friend) has become old.

confounding Destructive.

cruel knife Fine metaphor, continued in the next line, evocative not merely of time but of human wounding, or of the cutting down of plants.

My sweet love's beauty though my lover's life i.e. (he will not be taken from memory), for his beauty will survive even though he die.

black lines Of print; but perhaps *black* has also its sinister significance here.

still green i.e. always young.

Sonnet 64

Another sonnet on the theme of the ravages of time, but here much wider in scope than the previous one; the lines are almost overloaded with reference and association, though there is considerable duplication of the language and concepts of Sonnet 55. The significant difference of emphasis comes in the sestet, and particularly its concluding couplet. The poet, having contemplated thc effect of time on civilizations and on nature, is brought to feel 'That Time will come and take my love away'; the couplet does not speak of immorality through verse, but only of weeping and fear.

fell Ruthless.

the rich proud cost of buried outworn age The rich ostentation that has gone, the poor relics of the past.

down razed i.e. burnt down.

And brass eternal slave to mortal rage The destruction of death – the inscriptions on brasses, representative of civilization, are destroyed.

ocean ... kingdom Notice the switch to the natural effects of time while cunningly retaining the analogy of civilization and its destruction.

main Expanse.

Increasing store with loss ... store i.e. material taken from the sea with the incoming tide, and yet lost again when the tide turns.

interchange of state As usual in Shakespeare, 'state' carries overtones, and the interaction described is of changing conditions and of the great changes which destroy 'states'.

confounded to decay i.e. destroyed and left ruined.

to ruminate i.e. to consider carefully.

That Time will come Note the switch from the universal to the personal and human, a change expressive of pathos.

This thought is as a death ... it fears to lose Obviously the general meaning is that the thought of losing the beloved is a terrible one, but it cannot be ignored.

Sonnet 65

A continuation of the theme of the previous sonnet. The question asked is how beauty may survive the ravages of time, and there is much natural and storm imagery. The sonorous verse leads towards the inevitable (and perhaps comforting) conclusion that the immortality of his verse may preserve the beauty of his beloved.

sad mortality o'ersways their power i.e. destruction is all-powerful, and overcomes all other 'powers' (brass, stone, etc).

rage violence.

Whose action i.e. whose strength (to defend itself).

wrackful siege of battering days The analogy is with Nature, the storms that last long and wreck everything.

rocks impregnable Note the force obtained by the use of inverted word order.

Nor ... but time decays i.e. even steel gates succumb to the effects of time.

Shall Time's best jewel from Time's chest be hid? Complex construction – the best jewel is youth and beauty, which will ultimately be seized by Time and be stored in his chest.

his swift foot i.e. the onward quick movement of time.

his spoil of beauty i.e. his *des*poiling of beauty, his destruction of it.

have might i.e. power.

Sonnet 66

This sonnet is unusual in that some of the rhymes are trisyllables, rhyming only on the last syllable. It is also unusual in that ten of the fourteen lines begin with the word 'And'. This conjunction is used with rhetorical force, for the poem is a strong indictment of enumerated evils – evils so strongly felt, in fact, that the poet would wish to die rather than endure them. But there is one reservation – sounded in the couplets, the first line of which echoes the first line of the poem – if he quits life he quits his love, who would thus be left alone. The 'conceit' in this poem is therefore a listing of all the evils of life, a list which personifies them.

these i.e. the list of evil things which follows.

As to behold Desert a beggar born i.e. He who should be rewarded gets nothing.

needy nothing ... jollity A worthless person richly dressed.

And purest Faith ... forsworn i.e. loyalty or trust maliciously abused.

And gilded Honour ... misplac'd Position or status shamefully given to those undeserving of it.

And maiden Virtue ... strumpeted i.e. what is good abused or prostituted.
right Perfection True virtue, completeness of being.
Strength ... disabled i.e. true integrity undermined by those who hold the power, albeit temporarily.
Art i.e. art in the widest sense: man's achievements in the scientific and intellectual spheres. 'made tongue-tied' obviously suggests 'render impotent or inarticulate.'
Folly ... Doctor-like ... controlling skill Ignorance, behaving like a know-all, rules the really skilful.
simple Truth ... Simplicity i.e. what is obvious and right is abused, by dullness.
captive Good ... captain ill Antithesis: what is good is subordinated to what is evil.
Tir'd with all these Note the effectiveness of the repetition.
Save that to die Except that, if I die.

Sonnet 67

This sonnet starts by asking why the beloved should live in a world of corruption, and then goes on to indicate the nature of this vice. The second part of the octave takes up the idea that he will be imitated, that his beauty cannot be captured through the use of cosmetics, and that real beauty is the poorer beside him, and in fact lives upon 'his gains'. The couplet brings the conclusion that Nature keeps the beloved as proof in the evil future of what riches she once had.

infection The corruption which exists in life.
grace impiety (by his presence) shed goodness on what is evil.
lace itself i.e. ornament itself, show itself off.
false painting i.e. the use of cosmetics, much employed by Elizabethan courtiers. It has also been thought that this could well be a reference to the inferior verses of a rival poet.
dead seeming ... living hue i.e. the false effect as distinct from the real complexion.
poor beauty indirectly seek i.e. those of inferior attraction try

to imitate his beauty by trickery (painting), but that beauty is unique.

Beggar'd of blood ... gains i.e. nature lacks living vitality except what she gains from the friend, for though she has many children they do not yield her the beauty he does.

Oh him she stores ... bad i.e. she preserves him in order to show in an evil future what beauty she once possessed.

Sonnet 68

A continuation, and amplification, of the previous sonnet. The first few lines represent the natural beauty of the beloved, with another attack on those who with cosmetics try to emulate his beauty; the second part of the octave refers to the rather ghoulish practice of cutting the hair from the dead and putting it on the living, as wigs. The beloved needs no adornment, and the couplet to this sonnet comes to the same conclusion as that of the previous one – he is treasured by Nature, since he represents real beauty as distinct from 'false Art'.

the map The true picture of.

bastard signs i.e. cosmetic aids to a false beauty.

inhabit on a living brow i.e. the use of cosmetics on the face.

the right of sepulchres i.e. what ought to be buried with the corpse.

To live a second life ... dead fleece made another gay i.e. that hair taken from the dead was to be used again as a wig, and would make the second wearer attractive.

those holy antique hours Perhaps, the true beauty of the past.

it self and true i.e. beauty remains the same.

Making no summer i.e. not fashioning a false youth.

as for a map i.e. just as she would preserve a picture.

Sonnet 69

The opening describes the beloved's outward perfection, about which all are agreed; but there are those who praise him, who in fact look deeper. However, probably because of the baseness of their own characters, they cannot appreciate the beauty of the beloved's mind, as reflected in his actions. His actions are wilfully misjudged; and the last words of the sonnet are that the friend 'dost common grow' (the implication being, by associating with people of evil or commonplace minds).

Want nothing that the thought ... mend Lack nothing, so that no tactful allowances of kind hearts are needed to improve upon the friend's perfect attributes.
give thee that due i.e. acknowledge this.
even so as foes commend Just as enemies are fair.
outward praise i.e. what is said openly.
confound Destroy. See note p.65.
in guess The implication is, of course, that they guess wrongly.
Then, churls, their thoughts ... rank smell of weeds Their evil minds boorishly place a foul interpretation on your actions, in order to give you an unpleasant reputation.
But why thy odour matcheth not ... common grow These lines appear to mean that the poet considers that his friend's reputation does not square with his looks, since he has made himself common by mixing with all and sundry.

Sonnet 70

Again a continuation, with, at the beginning, an attack on slanderers. Beauty is always vulnerable, but the next section seems to imply that slander is subject to approval as well as condemnation, and that if the time is right slander will in fact be on your side. But the fact still remains that envy continues to grow against someone who enjoys a good reputation, and the friend is told that if he did not suffer some evil imputation he would indeed be unique.

thy defect i.e. your sin, your suffering.
mark i.e. object.

ornament ... suspect i.e. (beauty) is attended by suspicion.

A crow that flies i.e. suspicion.

So thou be good ... a pure unstained prime These obscure lines seem to mean that if you are good, slander will attempt to diminish you. But since you have now attained your prime, either having avoided being slandered or having proved your slanderers wrong, you have indeed triumphed. For you have survived your youth – your most vulnerable time, since 'canker vice the sweetest buds doth love.'

ambush of young days i.e. the dangers of youth.

Either ... charged Escaping assault, or victorious when attacked.

cannot be so thy praise i.e. cannot be merely praise (there is more to it than this).

To tie up envy, ever more enlarg'd i.e. jealousy cannot be restrained, but is always being turned loose.

some suspect of ill masked not thy show i.e. if you were not clouded by some suspicion of evil.

Then thou alone ... owe You would be remarkable in ruling whole kingdoms of hearts.

Sonnet 71

This moving sonnet strikes a new note, in that although death has been touched on before in the sequence, now the poet gives over the whole of the octave to enjoining his friend not to mourn for him when he is dead. The sestet returns to the poet's verses, but even if the friend should read them in the future he is conjured to 'let your love even with my life decay' lest he should be ridiculed.

surly sullen i.e. the heavy funeral (bell).

should make you woe i.e. should make you grieve.

rehearse i.e. repeat.

decay i.e. fall away, no longer exist.

with me i.e. with my love, our relationship.

Sonnet 72

The second direct injunction to forget him when he is gone, this time qualified by the idea that his friend could 'devise some virtuous lie', so that the poet's reputation might in this way be increased. But we detect some irony in this conception, which carries us through to the end of the octave. The sestet is a sustained expression of the poet's unworthiness, particularly the unworthiness of his verses.

task you to recite i.e. require you to list.
worthy prove i.e. provide evidence (of what merit I possessed).
virtuous lie i.e. a powerful or meritorious lie; or possibly one which demonstrated his virtues.
mine own desert i.e. what I truly deserved.
hang more praise i.e. credit me with more (after my death).
niggard truth i.e. grudging truth (would allow).
false ... untrue Note that these two lines are dependent for their effect on a play on words involving 'lying'.
My name My reputation.
to shame nor me nor you i.e. (and not survive) to bring shame on you, or on you for speaking well of me.
that which I bring forth i.e. his poems.
And so should you ... worth i.e. you would be made ashamed (by loving something worthless).

Sonnet 73

This depends for its effect on the control of the three quatrains that lead up to the couplet. The image of the opening lines is autumnal, the decline of the year approximating to the decline of life. This at once establishes a rather mournful tone, and this is extended with a kind of noble resignation in the second quatrain. The final section deals with night and the coming extinction of vitality in sleep on the one hand, and death on the other; with the couplet reminding the friend that he will soon have to forgo his love.

shake against the cold i.e. tremble with the coming of the cold.

Bare ruin'd choirs Apparently a comparison with ruined cathedrals provides the basis for this metaphor.

Death's second self that seals up i.e. sleep, but the image reflects the sealing of a coffin.

glowing ... ashes of his youth The image appears to convey the acceptance of the dying down of passion in middle life. It will completely cease to burn when death comes.

This thou perceiv'st The couplet acknowledges that his friend has been more loving since realizing that he is going to lose the love of the poet, who is soon to die.

Sonnet 74

A continuation of the theme of the last sonnet, though initially developed through law and legal imagery; his lines are again the central focus, since the friend can re-read these and take from them the poet's spirit. The sestet continues with death and the body, but then becomes almost too complex for analysis (though see notes below). The couplet again refers to the immortality of the verses, and thus of the poet, serving as an admirable contrast with the death imagery of the previous lines.

fell arrest Fierce seizure, death.

all bail i.e. any temporary relief.

in this line i.e. what I write here, and also the 'line' of succession to a property or an estate.

still 'Will ever be' (with you).

reviewest When you read this again.

review i.e. re-view, look at again.

The very part was consecrate to thee i.e. that was devoted to you.

earth ... spirit Deliberate contrast between the heavy and inanimate in death (the body) and the spirit, the essential being. His spirit survives in his verse.

the dregs of life i.e. the body.
The coward conquest of a wretch's knife Marlowe's murder, and the poet's thoughts of suicide have been put forward. But perhaps the 'wretch' is Death or Time.
Too base of thee ... remembered i.e. too low or unworthy for you to remember.
The worth of that ... remains i.e. my body's worth was my spirit: this has not perished, but lives on in my verse.

Sonnet 75

The theme is nourishment through the existence of the beloved, the initial comparison being with food and Nature. This is developed into the idea of joy in possession, with the poet's moods alternating between wishing to keep his beloved to himself and letting the world witness the beloved's beauty. These fluctuating emotions occupy the sestet too, with the beloved always the centre of life and love. The couplet climaxes the poem with the contrast between pining for his friend's presence, and feasting upon it.

sweet seasoned showers i.e. gentle and beneficent.
for the peace of you i.e. contentment in your company or love.
hold such strife i.e. I am in conflict (with myself).
proud as an enjoyer i.e. delighted in having you with me.
the filching age A comment on the times – the false times, dishonest, deceiving.
counting best i.e. thinking it preferable.
better'd i.e. being happy and exultant (that others may see how I delight in you).
starved i.e. longing for.
pine Starve.
or all away My delight all gone.

Sonnet 76

The basic theme here is the poet's own writing, and his lack of an adventurous spirit, or innovation, in composition. He also ponders on why he always writes on the same subject, his love, coming to the conclusion that all his writing is saying the same thing over again, with a concluding comparison with the sun and his love at the end.

barren of new pride i.e. devoid of fresh ornamentation.
variation or quick change The reference here is to the poet's feeling that his verse lacks variety, and that he is inexpert in the use of fashionable conceits.
with the time i.e. the current vogue.
new found methods i.e. new structures or ways of composition.
compounds strange i.e. outlandish coinages.
invention in a noted weed i.e. my rhetoric in the current, easily recognizable mode.
tell my name Reveals me.
where they did proceed i.e. from whence they came.
my argument My recurring theme.
dressing old words new i.e. saying again what I always say. The next line signifies the same.
already spent i.e. already finished.
For as the sun ... Just as the sun renews himself daily and appears to ascend and decline through the day, so is my verse a slight variation upon a familiar theme.

Sonnet 77

The poem opens with the idea of the mirror and the sundial providing means for showing the passage of time and the loss of youth, but the 'vacant leaves' of the third line seem to mean that the poet is presenting his friend with blank sheets, with the sonnet here as commentary. Next he returns to the mirror and the sundial, but then advises the friend to commit what 'thy memory cannot contain' to these pages. Developing an image, he says that these thoughts will be like children who grow up. The conceit is a curious one, but it is well-sustained.

how thy beauties wear i.e. how time is treating you.

Thy dial i.e. sundial.
The vacant leaves thy mind's imprint will bear i.e. because of the poet's injunction to his friend to make use of them.
this learning mayst thou taste i.e. this is what you will learn from it – a reference forward to the last four lines of the sonnet.
will truly show i.e. reveal accurately to you.
Of mouthed graves will give thee memory i.e. your mirror will bring to your mind the grave ready to receive you – for it will be obvious that you are growing old.
shady stealth i.e. the shadows.
Look what i.e. consider.
these waste blanks i.e. these empty sheets.
Those children nurs'd, deliver'd from thy brain i.e. (your thoughts) will be like children brought up by a nurse.
To take a new acquaintance of thy mind They will later seem to you to be more significant (just like children who grow up and prove capable of more than we have imagined).
These offices This can only be a reference to the mirror and the sundial as recording the effects of time – perhaps the implication is that when the friend refers to them he will himself be measuring the experience which enriches the book.

Sonnet 78

An address yet again to the beloved, but with some reference to a rival bard's usurping the poet's position. He then proceeds to enumerate exactly what his beloved has achieved through his charm, but returns to his own achievements through the love of his friend, asserting that his are more complete than the efforts of others. The Sonnet is full of ironic self-deprecation.

have I invok'd thee i.e. the friend.
fair assistance The meaning appears to be 'inspiration'.
every alien pen hath got my use i.e. strangers have adopted my habit of writing about you.
And under thee their poesy disperse And spread their poetry under the protection of your patronage.

the dumb i.e. the poet himself (see line 14).
on high Loudly.
heavy ignorance Another modest reference to himself. (Again see line 14.)
added feathers to the learned's wing i.e. helped the learned (possibly the rival poet).
Whose influence is thine i.e. you have inspired me.
mend the style i.e. improve it, perhaps 'are an ornament' to it.
And arts ... be Learning, culture, gains from your gracious patronage.
But thou art all my art Punning phrase – I give all my skill to you – you are all my learning.
As high as learning ... ignorance My rough lack of knowledge is lifted into knowledge by you.

Sonnet 79

Now the poet's place has gone to another, but the sonnet goes on to argue that any poet writing of the friend 'steals' something from him and can never in fact exceed the virtue of the original. There is much play on the words 'owes' and 'pay'.

whilst I alone i.e. when I was the only one (writing about you).
thy gentle grace i.e. displayed all your beauty and your patronage.
gracious The word has been picked up from the previous line – 'my elegant verses are not as good as they were, and in any case they are out of favour with you' seems to be the burthen of the rest of the line.
my sick Muse ... place i.e. I have to yield up what I enjoyed to others.
thy lovely argument Elliptical construction: 'my setting forth of your virtues'.
travail i.e. labour, dedication.
what of thee thy poet doth invent i.e. what virtues are found by whoever writes about you.

He robs . . . thee again i.e. he takes it from you . . . and repays you (in verse).
lends thee virtue i.e. endows you with virtue.
afford i.e. allow.
owes . . . pay i.e. you reward him merely by being his patron.

Sonnet 80

Again the tone involves an apparent denigration of self; the poet feels that a finer poet is writing of his friend, but can only describe his own efforts as 'saucy' by comparison with those of the more gifted. The central metaphor, which is sustained through part of the octave and all the sestet, is that of a small boat (the poet's talent), his rival's being of 'tall building and of goodly pride'. (This has, however, been pointed out as a possible allusion to what the 'saucy barks' of the English did against the 'goodly pride' of the Armada.)

how I faint i.e. lose hope.
better spirit i.e. a more complete poet.
spends all his might i.e. employs all his poetic powers.
to make me tongue-tied i.e. to render my poems inarticulate.
your worth, wide as the ocean i.e. since you have great generosity of spirit.
My saucy bark My impudent little craft.
broad main i.e. wide expanse. (Refers back to line 5.)
wilfully i.e. boldly but misguidedly.
shallowest i.e. smallest. (A comparison here too to the respective draughts of large and small vessels.)
soundless deep i.e. in the unfathomed ocean.
tall building . . . goodly pride i.e. having a towering superstructure . . . of massive bulk.
he thrive i.e. the other poet.
my love was my decay i.e. it was my love for you that brought me to this.

Sonnet 81

A return to a well-worn theme – the theme of death and the immortality of the friend through the poet's verses. It begins interestingly with a double 'or': the question is whether the poet will survive to write his friend's epitaph or whether he will die before his friend. This heralds yet another exploration of immortality.

Or Whether.
From hence i.e. from this life.
from hence i.e. from now on, a deliberate twisting of the above sense.
once gone i.e. having died.
a common grave Not literally; the phrase means 'I shall be forgotten'.
entombed in men's eyes i.e. your grave (by comparison) will be where all can see it (and appreciate your worth).
my gentle verse i.e. his poems – the real monument referred to in the previous lines.
not yet created i.e. future generations.
your being shall rehearse i.e. will talk of you.
virtue i.e. ability (to immortalize).
in the mouths of men i.e. they will speak of you, having read what I have written about you.

Sonnet 82

This praises the friend's beauty of mind as well as of appearance, but again bemoans the inadequacy of his own poetry, which is being surpassed in these 'time-bettering days'. In the sestet the poet praises himself somewhat for telling the truth about his beloved and not straining after effect, a practice that could not do justice to the beloved, whose beauty and worth are above such devices.

I grant thou were not ... Muse i.e. you are not tied to my verses alone.

without attaint O'erlook i.e. you can read without any sense of shame.
dedicated Devoted.
as fair in knowledge as in hue Just as your presence is good, so is your judgement.
Finding thy worth ... praise i.e. you are too eminent for me to be the only one to praise you.
fresher stamp of the time-bettering days This appears to be ironical, or it may be just self-deprecation; it means 'an image of you made by the advance poetry of these times'.
truly sympathiz'd i.e. correctly, rightly represented.
true plain words i.e. reflecting honesty, integrity and lack of ornamentation.
gross painting i.e. exaggerated representation.
Where cheeks need blood i.e. to deck out an anaemic personality.

Sonnet 83

The first four lines are written in praise of the friend's qualities, which need no adornment; the second four lines mention the poet's not having written lately about the friend. The sestet registers the fact that the friend has blamed him for this, but that, in fact, the poet's silence is itself a tribute – others desecrate his friend's beauty by poor writing but the poet has chosen to remain dumb. The friend's beauty is greater than anything that can be written about it.

to your fair no painting set i.e. and so I embellished your beauty not at all.
The barren tender i.e. arid writing.
a poet's debt i.e. to his friend.
slept in your report I was sluggish in singing your praises.
being extant i.e. still living.
a modern quill i.e. an ordinary pen (a reference to the commonplace quality of the poetry written about his friend).
came too short i.e. be inadequate.

you did impute i.e. you thought this silence sinful in me.
being dumb i.e. because I was silent.
For I impair not i.e. I do not damage your beauty (by being silent).
would give life and bring a tomb i.e. want to immortalize him, but extinguish him through their lack of skill.
both your poets That is, Shakespeare and another; or two other poets.

Sonnet 84

The greatest praise that can be given to the friend is that he *is*, and is the most perfect of specimens. Generally poets write in order to extol their subject, but he who writes of the friend has merely to copy the perfection of his original. Such a poet will make his own reputation if he copies what is perfection; the couplet, however, adds to this, for it suggests that the friend is fond of being praised, or of giving indiscriminate praise.

that says most The word-play really means 'Who is there writing who can say more than this?'
immured i.e. walled in. (Latin: *murus*, a wall.)
should example i.e. could cite (such an equal).
penury ... pen Obvious punning, embracing the poverty of the writing and the fact that the friend's beauty is 'penned up' within him.
That you ... his story By confining his subject to you, *ipso facto* improves it.
so clear i.e. perfect.
counterpart Picture.
shall fame his wit i.e. make his talents famous.
your beauteous blessings i.e. those qualities with which you are blessed.
Being fond ... praises worse This probably means that since he is over-fond of praise he receives much fulsome flattery.

Sonnet 85

The idea of the first four lines is that the poet himself is decorously silent, though others write extravagantly of his friend. He merely thinks 'good thoughts', though he endorses all such praises. His own words he feels to be inferior to those of others, but his love for his friend takes precedence above all. He prefers to dwell on the quality of the love in his 'dumb thoughts'.

in manners keeps her still i.e. holds back with deference.
comments ... compiled The implication is that others write elaborate compositions in praise of the friend.
Reserve their character Retain their style.
by all the Muses fil'd Drawn from the great poets.
unletter'd clerk i.e. the parish clerk who uttered the responses.
To every hymn ... affords He echoes the praises of talented writers.
In polish'd form ... pen Written in the best possible way.
Though words come hindmost ... before Although my writing is inferior, my love is of superior worth.
for the breath of words respect i.e. pay attention to others for their words.
speaking in effect This is another couplet concluding in word-play: the meaning here is, 'truly, my thoughts are eloquent'.

Sonnet 86

This deals directly with the lure of the rival poet who seeks his friend's love, or affection or patronage. The quatrains of the octave are couched in rhetorical questions, the imagery of sailing being predominant in the first, and perhaps a suggestion of supernatural aid in the second. The contention is that the other poet's borrowings are responsible for his success, but the writer says that none of this worried him until he saw his friend's approval of his rival.

proud full sail Note the effect of stateliness in the image.

ripe thoughts in my brain inhearse Note the growth and death imagery in the same line – to 'inhearse' is to 'bury', as the word suggests.

their tomb the womb Note the internal rhyme and the continuance of the image of extinction.

spirit, by spirits ... write Difficult; perhaps his abilities receive supernatural aid; or perhaps the reference is to the great writers of the past. The pun is obvious.

pitch i.e. height.

nor his compeers by night Again the reference appears to be to the supernatural, perhaps the aid of great minds of the past.

my verse astonished i.e. petrified my writing.

affable familiar ghost i.e. his rival's chief support (supernatural or otherwise).

gulls Feeds or, possibly, deceives, misleads.

intelligence Information.

countenance i.e. approval or blessing, with a possible pun on countenance, beauty in the sense of (beautiful) features.

that enfeebled mine i.e. the knowledge (that you favoured him) made my own verse the poorer.

Sonnet 87

The first quatrain is a freeing of the friend from any bond or obligations towards the poet. The legal imagery is extended in the second quatrain to embrace the reversion of all the interest that the latter has in his friend back to him by deed of right. The octave labours the fact that originally the friend was guilty of misjudgement in his choice, but the poet comforts himself in the knowledge that at least he has possessed him in the past.

Thou art too dear i.e. above me, of nobler rank.

estimate i.e. your own worth.

charter The privilege, the rights.

releasing i.e. exemption.

determinate i.e. come to an end.

where is my deserving? How can I possibly deserve you?

my patent ... is swerving My rights (in you) revert to you.
mistaking i.e. crediting me with more than I deserved.
So thy great gift, upon misprision growing i.e. your love, based on an error of judgement.
Comes home again ... making On further consideration, your love returns to you – perhaps with the implication that it should be given to someone more worthy of it.
as a dream doth flatter i.e. as one is mighty in a dream.
in sleep a king The poet himself is a king when asleep.

Sonnet 88

There is a forward-looking, rather self-pitying note in the first quatrain, to the effect that in future should the poet's virtues be underrated by his friend; the poet will himself join in the friend's attack. He argues that he knows his own limitations well, and can therefore speak in support of his friend's reasons for disowning him. The sestet continues this theme, the poet concluding that he will be helping himself by showing his love for his friend in this way. The couplet is the conclusion to all this, in which the poet takes all the blame. There is rich word-play but little elevation in the tone of this sonnet.

to set me light i.e. to value me but little.
place my merit ... scorn i.e. expose my talents to public condemnation.
forsworn i.e. false, disloyal (obviously to the poet's love).
Upon thy part ... story I can give an account that supports yours.
attainted i.e. soiled, contaminated.
bending all my loving thoughts i.e. concentrating all my deep love.
The injuries My shortcomings.
Doing thee vantage ... me Subtle word-play: 'In serving you there is gain to myself and to you: to you because you have got rid of someone unworthy, to me because I can show my love by helping you in this' – this is a rough paraphrase of a complex expression.

That for thy right ... wrong To see that you are 'in the right' I will take all the blame.

Sonnet 89

The subject of the last sonnet is extended here, the poet thinking of occasions when the friend could leave him, or speak ill of him; knowing his limitations, he would acquiesce. He is prepared to suffer absence and to cease speaking the beloved's name, rather than to let him down by speaking of their past. The couplet implies the extreme of self-criticism and self-denial in order to preserve his friend's reputation.

fault i.e. sin.
comment i.e. elaborate, make it worse.
will halt i.e. cause myself to limp (in order to prove the truth of what you have said).
disgrace me half so ill i.e. discredit me falsely.
To set a form upon desired change i.e. to bring about, or set the seal upon, the changed relationship that you desire.
As I'll disgrace myself ... will i.e. as I will dishonour myself, knowing that you wish it.
I will acquaintance strangle and look strange i.e. I will end our (outward) relationship and 'cut' you.
Be absent from thy walks i.e. avoid your usual 'haunts'.
too much profane i.e. being too careless of speech.
haply Perhaps, by chance.
against ... debate i.e. I'll conquer my own wishes.
ne'er love him i.e. himself.

Sonnet 90

The opening lines invite the friend to hate him now (if hate he must), while everything else is going wrong for him. The sestet conveys his wish to have the hardest blow first; the climaxing couplet explains that thus all other troubles coming later will seem as nothing.

While the world is bent my deeds to cross While everyone, (and everything) else goes against me.
And do not drop in for an after-loss There is some obscurity here; the line probably means 'Do not subject me to a later tragedy or suffering'.
hath 'scaped i.e. has recovered from.
rearward ... conquer'd The sequence is a military one of attack and repulse – the meaning is 'do not come afterwards when I have got over my grief'.
To linger out i.e. stretch out, protract.
other petty griefs i.e. small sadnesses (by comparison with the major one of his friend forsaking him).
in the onset At the beginning, the first assault (the military imagery still being continued).
first ... worst ... Fortune's Note the internal rhyme, and the submission to the will of fate.
strains of woe i.e. types of sadness.

Sonnet 91

The first four lines are cumulative, the poet considering a number of things which give different people their greatest pleasure. But by the beginning of the sestet he is asserting what pleases him most; the enjoyment of his friend's love. This final section cleverly echoes the first in its analogies, but ends with the realization he might lose his friend's love and be brought to despair.

skill i.e. intellectual talent.
though new-fangled ill Modish but ugly clothes.
humour ... adjunct pleasure i.e. each particular nature has its corresponding desire.
But these particulars are not my measure These things (listed above in the sonnet) are no pleasure to me.
I better in one general best i.e. I find all these petty perfections in one perfect person.
high birth ... wealth ... garments ... hawks A reference back to the first quatrains.

Wretched . . . wretched Note the deliberate repetition to underline the abjectness of the poet's threatened future.

Sonnet 92

The theme here is that whatever the friend does, as long as the poet lives he will love him; should the friend reject that love, he will no longer find life possible. He feels that coldness from his friend could bring about his death; thus he will not live to see his own outright rejection. The octave therefore concentrates on expressing his own happiness in love, and his consequent happiness in death should that love once change. The couplet brings an enigmatic ending to the poem – the fact that what appears so beautiful (his friend) may be false without his knowledge.

term of life . . . assured i.e. guaranteed to me as long as I live.
the worst of wrongs . . . the least of them A contrast between the most terrible calamity that could occur – his rejection by the friend – and the common possibilities of distance or coldness.
humour Nature.
inconstant mind . . . revolt Your changing whims . . . inconstancy.
happy title Probably it is best defined by the idea of 'blessing' or 'good fortune'.
so blessed fair . . . blot So beautiful as to be immaculate.

Sonnet 93

Here the poet hints at his disquiet when he compares himself to a deceived husband. He still believes himself loved while the friend could now be in love with another – because his beloved's sweet face could never reveal 'the false heart's history', no matter what his real feelings might be. The couplet carries overtones of suspected corruption in its mention of the beauty of Eve's apple.

love's face i.e. the face that love puts on, outward show.
alter'd new i.e. recently changed.
In many's looks i.e. in the looks of many.
should nothing thence ... tell Would reveal nothing but harmony.
If thy sweet virtue answer not thy show If you are not as virtuous as you look.

Sonnet 94

A difficult poem, with perhaps a deliberate ambiguity which makes exact interpretation elusive. The first quatrain appears to mean that there are people who have the power to cause injury to others, but they do not choose to use it; they are capable of influencing others while themselves remaining uninfluenced. He goes on to say that these men are in fact their own masters and rightly fortunate, whereas others are caretakers of their souls. The sestet pursues the analogy with Nature; flowers have their own beauty, but can become diseased; then the weed makes a more beautiful show than they do. The couplet continues the analogy by saying that that which is beautiful but corrupted is far worse than anything that is basically impure. The difficulty in this well-balanced sonnet is that the first part can be taken both as eulogy ('They rightly do inherit heaven's graces') and indictment ('are themselves as stone/Unmoved, cold'). This is an intentional ambiguity, reflecting the conflict in Shakespeare's feelings about the quality and character of his beloved, who must have inspired the poem.

they most do show i.e. what they threaten to do.
and to temptation slow This implies rectitude, but there is something inhuman about it too.
rightly Certainly.
husband nature's riches from expense i.e. preserve what they have.
Others but stewards This appears to mean that some are merely ostentatious, with no inner strength.

Though to itself it only live and die Here we touch an early theme again, the idea of failing to perpetuate the species.
outbraves his dignity i.e. makes a more impressive appearance.
turn sourest by their deeds i.e. by their own corruption.
fester Rot.

Sonnet 95

This is a sonnet warning against the loss of reputation and the possibility of corruption within the friend's great physical beauty. Again the analogy is with Nature, the canker-worm which destroys the bud of the rose. His name dignifies the most ribald tale, yet the warning is reiterated by the close of the poem; his friend's beauty may save him for the present, but 'Constant dripping wears away stone'.

spot i.e. stain, corrupt.
budding name Note the extension of the floral image. The meaning is 'youthful reputation'.
what sweets i.e. virtue, fine qualities.
That tongue Rumour, or perhaps the work of another poet.
lascivious ... sport i.e. sneers at your promiscuity.
dispraise i.e. lower your reputation.
Naming ... blesses an ill report Merely by speaking of you, one dignifies an unpleasant rumour.
mansion i.e. outward appearance.
every blot i.e. sign of corruption.
this large privilege i.e. the good fortune of possessing such beauty, for which many allowances are made.
The hardest knife ill-us'd ... edge i.e. anything continually overworked suffers: the power of friction or erosion.

Sonnet 96

The poem deals with reports of the beloved, and comes to the conclusion by the end of the octave that everything about his friend's conduct can palliate vice – he 'makes faults graces'. The sestet opens with the analogy of the wolf disguised as a lamb, and refers back to the friend by saying the latter could similarly lead people astray if he so wished. The couplet, which also concludes Sonnet 36, asserts that the poet will guard his, the friend's, reputation.

wantonness Self-indulgence, particularly in the sexual sense.
gentle sport See note p.76.
Both grace and faults ... more or less Your natural attractions excuse your errors, and such are your attractions that you make faults appear attractive.
basest jewel i.e. one of least value.
To truths translated and for true things deem'd Accepted as a moral code, judged to be right.
his looks translate i.e. transform or change his appearance.
gazers ... away Admirers ... astray.
the strength of all thy state i.e. the many attractions you possess.
But do not so report See our note, p.43. These lines are an exact repetition of the last two lines of Sonnet 36.

Sonnet 97

This reverts to the nature-imagery characteristic of some of the earlier sonnets. Here the language simultaneously evokes deprivation and consummation, the seeming paradox pointed by the seasons' changes. The sonnet has a consistency of mood – desolation in the beloved's absence.

How like a winter ... been The reference is to the effect of physical absence – or it might merely be to disagreement, spiritual alienation.
the pleasure of the fleeting year The enduring happiness of his friend's presence, compared with the impermanence of the natural seasons of the year.
this time remov'd was summer's time The expression of an ironic fact – the time of absence, though like a winter, occurred in the real season of summer.

The teeming autumn ... increase i.e. the last line's summer, merging into harvest-time.

the wanton burthen of the prime i.e. the new growth of spring, or perhaps the birth of children (conceived in high summer).

Like widow'd wombs after their lords' decease i.e. the birth of posthumous children – a superbly condensed expression. The comparison is with the beloved's absence (like death) and the richness of the season (like birth).

abundant issue ... unfather'd fruit i.e. a prolific increase would seem as nothing, with the beloved absent.

with so dull a cheer i.e. dismally.

That leaves took pale As in late autumn – a further extension of the poet's melancholy mood.

Sonnet 98

Another evocation of Nature-melancholy. Spring and summer provide the main description, but they also reflect the poet's mood of blind melancholy because of the beloved's absence. Again the analogy with winter is drawn in the climactic couplet.

Have I been absent in the spring This obviously refers back to the summer/autumn absence in Sonnet 97. And the use here of the past imperfect tense of the verb 'to be' makes one think there may have been more than one spring absence ('have ... been' rather than 'was').

proud-pied A fine double-barrelled coinage, meaning 'many-coloured'.

trim i.e. clothes (continuing the personification of April).

That heavy Saturn laugh'd The idea is that the melancholy mood lifts in the joy of spring. The reference is to astrology and the 'dull' planet Saturn.

lays Songs.

make me any summer's story tell i.e. (I could not) write about the beauties of summer.

proud lap i.e. the ground, the beautiful beds where they were to be found. (Matthew Arnold's 'cool, flowery lap of earth').

figures of delight i.e. symbolic of beauty.
Drawn after you ... those They are modelled on your beauty, and you are the symbol of them all.

Sonnet 99

This is a 'sonnet' of fifteen lines, there being three 'a' rhymes in the 'octave'; the sestet is regular. The theme is again developed though Nature, being this time a cataloguing of flowers, all poor compared with the beloved. The extra line upsets the balance somewhat, and the conceit is much more contrived than hitherto in this sequence.

forward i.e. early.
The purple pride i.e. beauty.
thy soft cheek The reference is to the flower.
grossly Coarsely.
The lily ... hand The lily had stolen the pallor of your hand.
The roses fearfully They are guilty (because they too have taken from the beloved).
blushing shame ... white despair The first rose is blushing because it has stolen from the beloved, the second is in despair because it can never equal him.
annex'd thy breath i.e. stolen (the sweetness of) your breath.
canker i.e. the canker-worm (destroyed him).
sweet Fragrance.

Sonnet 100

Self-recrimination, for long neglecting to write of his beloved; a desire also to return to the one subject that provides him with his being and his inspiration. The role of the poet is considered in the sestet, with the couplet referring specifically to the need to perpetuate the beloved's 'fame'.

all thy might i.e. strength of inspiration.
Spend'st i.e. dissipate.

Darkening thy power Abusing your strength.
That doth thy lays esteem i.e. that praises your songs.
skill and argument i.e. art and content.
resty i.e. inactive.
Time ... graven This marks the return to an earlier theme and image in the sonnets.
be a satire to decay i.e. hold decay up to ridicule.
Time's spoils i.e. what Time has captured.
So thou prevent'st ... knife Both the effects of Time (age) and the injuries (e.g. loss of vitality and beauty, disease), which Time inflicts as we get older.

Sonnet 101

This is another invocation to his Muse, which has again been charged with neglect. Perhaps his excuse must be that beauty, because it exists complete, requires no further justification, no adornment or decoration through verse. In the sestet the poet argues that nevertheless the 'Muse' must provide the record of the beloved's beauty for succeeding ages, the couplet rounding this off neatly.

truth in beauty dyed i.e. virtue *and* beauty.
on my love depends i.e. truth, and beauty depend on my friend.
and therein dignified You (the 'Muse') are elevated (by the beauty of the friend).
his colour fix'd i.e. set.
beauty's truth to lay No brush to put on (the paint).
intermix'd i.e. mixed, diluted.
for it lies in thee ... tomb i.e. you can give him fame beyond death.
outlive a gilded tomb i.e. outlive, survive death (with reference to an ornate family grave).
do thy office i.e. perform what is your duty, your function.
long hence as he shows now To appear to the future generations as he is now.

Sonnet 102

Again in the first part the emphasis is on silence or lack of self-advertisement. He refers back to their early love and the poems that chronicled it, dying away in maturity. The sestet elaborates the parallel already made of poet and nightingale; the bird does not sing all the time – hence the poet's excuse for his own recent silence now their love is no longer new and 'in the spring'.

in seeming What it appears to be.
less the show appear i.e. there is less evidence (of my love).
merchandiz'd i.e. cheapened in the selling.
esteeming i.e. worth.
doth publish i.e. speak loudly of.
was wont i.e. used to.
Philomel The nightingale. (Philomela was raped by Tereus, her brother-in-law, who cut out her tongue to prevent her exposing him. She exacted her revenge, and was later changed into a nightingale.)
in summer's front i.e. early in the summer.
stops her pipe in growth of riper days i.e. ceases to sing as the summer wears on.
mournful hymns did hush the night i.e. her sad (but beautiful) songs caused all other creatures to be silent.
wild music The variety of birdsong.
burthens Burdens.
sweets Beautiful things.
dear delight i.e. precious.
like her i.e. the nightingale.
not dull you i.e. deaden your feelings.

Sonnet 103

Again the focus is on the beloved friend, the argument in the first few lines being that he is in need of no adornment. The second quatrain asserts that he can easily see his superiority to what is written about him by looking in the mirror. The sestet elaborates this, implying that verse might spoil the image of the beloved, since the writing falls so far short of its subject's perfection.

what poverty i.e. inferior work.
The argument all bare i.e. the theme, the beloved himself.
over-goes my blunt invention i.e. outdistances my dull images.
Dulling my lines i.e. depriving them of vivacity.
striving to mend, to mar A play on words; here the meaning is: 'trying to improve upon is to spoil'.
no other pass i.e. (I have) no other object.
in my verse can sit i.e. can be found in my writing.

Sonnet 104

A fine sonnet in which the poet celebrates his concept of the permanence of his friend's youthful beauty. The span of time mentioned is three years, and again rich use is made of natural imagery. The poem is full of poignant recall and, in the sestet, of apprehension of the future changes in the appearance of the beloved. The couplet conveys the idea that future generations will lose by not seeing that perfect beauty. The effects are achieved largely through the descriptions, the repetition and the felicitous use of phrase, the poignant treatment of the eternal temporal theme.

when first your eye I eyed Obvious word-play, but with an idea of seeing, and being aware of, beauty directly.
three summers' pride i.e. leaves, the panoply of trees.
fresh ... green i.e. youthful, and still youthful.
Ah yet doth beauty ... hand Time moves on like the hand of a clock and unperceived by us.
sweet hue Your good looks.
methinks still doth stand It seems to me that you are still the same.

Hath notion i.e. is subject to change.

For fear of this . . . dead The construction of the last two lines is difficult. They mean, 'I am fearful that, because of these changes, coming generations will never have seen perfect beauty'.

Sonnet 105

The poet, sensitively aware that his love might be called 'idolatry', provides his own definition of the beloved object – 'Fair, kind, and true' – which affords him 'three themes in one'. There, obviously, all these qualities are to be found.

as an idol show i.e. appear to be worshipped.

Since all alike . . . be All my poems express the same caution, this love of mine.

Kind is my love . . . kind i.e. his attitude does not change.

Still constant in a wondrous excellence i.e. he is always the same, in appearance and in virtue.

One thing expressing, leaves out difference Because I am always writing on the same theme, I deliberately omit other themes ('difference').

varying to other words i.e. perhaps displaying nuances within this chosen theme.

And in this change is my invention spent i.e. I devote all my energies to working out such variations on my theme.

Three themes in one As one critic has observed, there is here a religious association with the Holy Trinity.

wondrous scope i.e. expansive treatment.

Which three till now . . . one i.e. all these excellencies are to be found in the beloved – something never before known.

Sonnet 106

Here the poet contemplates the past, with particular reference to the poems of bygone ages and the people described in them. He feels the old bards would have liked to record the unsurpassed beauty of his friend, and in the sestet he comes to the conclusion that all past praises are really prophecies of the beauty to come – the beauty of his beloved. The couplet asserts that present-day writers cannot possibly do justice to such grace.

chronicle of wasted time i.e. the literature of the past.
wights People.
And beauty making beautiful old rhyme i.e. the poems are rendered beautiful through the qualities of the people they celebrated.
the blazon The setting forth or publishing (of beauty).
their antique pen would have express'd i.e. the old writers would have wished (to describe beauty such as yours).
Even . . . master now i.e. such beauty as you are master of, your own charms.
prefiguring Forecasting, presaying.
with divining eyes i.e. seeing into the future.
skill i.e. talent.
Have eyes to wonder . . . praise i.e. we can gaze wonderingly at your beauty, but there is now no one capable of doing it justice in verse.

Sonnet 107

A very difficult sonnet. There is an overall mood of melancholy; but the poet expresses his love for his friend through the immortality of the verse in which he celebrates him. Once more, the passage of time is the argument's core, with a number of fascinating allusions that provided commentators with somewhat bewildering clues in their attempts to date the sonnets. This is not our concern here, though the notes below will indicate some of the areas covered. The sestet is much concerned with death, over which poetry makes it possible to triumph.

Not mine own fears ... my true love control Neither the poet's own fears nor the accepted ideas of the world – which believes that love can last but a limited time – can set a date for the ending of his love (i.e. which will be never).

forfeit ... confin'd doom This probably means the penalty of mortal life or judgement.

the mortal moon eclipse endur'd There have been many attempts to explain this famous line. Some have detected a reference to the Armada (maintaining that it sailed in a crescent formation, though others have denied this); but it could be a reference to the Queen's recovery from an illness, or victory over a rebellion. Or even a lunar eclipse could be meant (there was one in 1595).

the sad augurs mock their own presage i.e. those who prophesied gloom (now that things are well) can but make light of their own forecasts.

Incertainties ... assur'd i.e. security has succeeded doubts.

olives of endless age i.e. a period of lasting peace. Again this has been associated with the defeat of the Armada.

balmy i.e. healthful, healing.

My love looks fresh i.e. my love (for the friend) springs up again.

death to me subscribes i.e. gives in.

insults o'er dull and speechless tribes i.e. triumphs over those who are apathetic and inarticulate – the general mass of people.

are spent i.e. are ended, finished.

Sonnet 108

A poem with expressions of constancy in love, but lamenting the difficulty of finding a new way to express that love's permanence. The second quatrain dwells on the perennial nature of a love which seems always new, even in the utterance, while the sestet perhaps asserts the idea that love triumphs over even the demands and tribulations of age.

may character i.e. represent in writing.
figur'd to thee my true spirit i.e. shown you my constancy.
register Set down.
prayers divine i.e. regular praying.
old thing old This probably means that, though their love is of some duration, the poet can still find the old vows and praises fresh and new.
I hallow'd thy fair name i.e. when first I wrote verse in worship of you.
So that eternal love ... dead These are the difficult lines; a possible paraphrase is: 'Eternal love, vigorously expressed, takes small account of the changes wrought by time, but instead makes old age its servant. It finds still in an old face the life of love, though, if on one judged by outward show, love might be thought to have ended.'

Sonnet 109

This asserts his own constancy in absence, for always his love returns to its resting-place, to his friend. The sestet develops the theme that whatever the poet's sins, he could never leave the source of all good, his friend. The couplet uses the symbol of the rose for the beloved – 'my all', the world's fine flower.

my flame to qualify To lessen my passion.
rang'd i.e. travelled widely, gone here and there.
Just ... exchang'd i.e. punctually.
bring water for my stain i.e. to cleanse myself of my guilt.
All frailties Weaknesses.
all kinds of blood People of differing temperaments.
preposterously In such an extreme form.
for nothing all thy sum of good The implication is 'to throw away your goodness for nothing'.
my rose i.e. my one and only beautiful beloved.

Sonnet 110

A celebrated sonnet admitting that he had cheapened himself in the past; but claiming that his love for his friend was always present. This in fact, with some elaboration, forms the major part of the octave. The opening is conversational, yet sonorous and moving.

a motley i.e. a clown.
Gor'd mine own thoughts A reference to the pieces of material in a clown's costume referred to as 'gores', though it could also have the more obvious meaning of 'savaged'.
Made old offences . . . new i.e. behaved badly by having new 'affections' – thus proving his inconstancy to the beloved.
look'd on truth . . . strangely i.e. been inconstant, averse to 'truth'.
These blenches gave my heart another youth But these turnings aside in fact gave me a greater love (for you).
worse essays i.e. even worse offences.
have what shall have no end A reference to the undying nature of the poet's love.
Mine appetite . . . an older friend I will not abuse you by testing my desires on others.
A god in love . . . confin'd This indicates the elevation of the friend – to whom he is restricted – above all others in the poet's mind.
next my heaven the best Outside of Heaven (the afterlife) you are my next best – i.e. all to me on earth.

Sonnet 111

This sonnet is obviously connected with the previous one – the poet lays the blame for his bad behaviour on Fortune, which has served him ill, by placing him in surroundings where he learned 'public manners' – i.e. coarser ones than his friend's. The second part of the octave shows that he feels he has become contaminated by the life he has led; but he believes that the pity of his friend – his sympathy – will cure him.

chide Blame.

my harmful deeds i.e. my capacity to do wrong.

public means ... public manners i.e. Fortune has made me dependent on the whim of the public, so that (in my work) I have to degrade myself.

a brand i.e. a particular mark; I am described in such a way.

is subdued i.e. (my real self) is subordinated.

like the dyer's hand i.e. which takes on the colour it is using.

Potions of eisel Vinegar.

Nor double penance to correct correction I will not refuse double penance, being twice corrected.

Sonnet 112

The poet takes great comfort from his friend's 'love and pity', and he reveals his reliance on the latter's tolerance. The second quatrain further develops this dependence, while the sestet stresses that he values no one else, and is completely wrapped up in the beloved. There are rare moments of bathos in this sonnet, and some clumsy constructions.

the impression fill i.e. make up for the wounds (I have received).

vulgar scandal Common gossip.

who calls me well or ill Who gives me a good or bad reputation.

o'er-green i.e. conceal (as scarred earth is covered by fresh green growth).

To know my shames or praises from your tongue i.e. 'to learn from you what I have done that is shameful, and what praiseworthy.

None else to me ... right or wrong i.e. no one else exists for me, neither do I exist for them in such a way as to alter my habits.

In so profound abysm ... voices Again, difficult. It seems to mean 'I lose all sense of everyone else, do not listen to their opinions'. 'My adder's sense' probably means shutting out the noise of (adders were traditionally deaf).

with my neglect I do dispense I explain my indifference to.
in my purpose bred i.e. so much part of my life.
That all the world . . . dead That everyone else is dead as far as I am concerned.

Sonnet 113

Again a reference to absence, with the poet now focusing on what he sees, or rather describing how he sees very little except what is within his mind – that is, the image of his friend. Whatever he sees is informed by that image; thus all outward images are false, since what the eye pictures within is the image of the beloved.

governs me i.e. moves me.
part Divides.
Seems seeing . . . out The poet's eye appears to see, but does not do so in reality.
latch i.e. register in the heart (or mind).
Of his quick objects . . . part i.e. what is seen at the moment is fleeting, the eye is one thing, the brain another.
holds what it doth catch This reinforces the last line: the eye does not retain what it sees.
rud'st Coarsest.
sweet favour i.e. attractive, blessed.
to your feature i.e. your form, or appearance or face – in fact, it makes them in your image.
Incapable of more Powerless to grasp anything further.
My most true mind . . . true Considerable word-play here: the constancy of my mind, the accuracy of my mind's eye, makes my outward eye false, since what it sees (is replaced by you in my mind).

Sonnet 114

Another sonnet that looks back to its predecessor. The debate is once more between the functions and representations of the outward and the inward eye. The tone is undistinguished and somewhat obscure.

Or whether . . . crown'd with you Is it that (my mind is full of you)?
the monarch's plague, this flattery The latter is 'deception', and the image is continued from the previous line.
this alchemy This is qualified in the next lines – so transforming objects that they all look like the friend. The reference back to the previous sonnet is obvious. The significance of the 'alternatives' in this first quatrain is, then, 'Is this mere flattery or deception, or is it true alchemy?'
monsters Grotesque creatures or objects
indigest Chaotic.
every bad a perfect best i.e. making of everything bad something perfect and complete.
As fast as objects . . . assemble The eye seeing things as perfectly put together.
'tis flattery in my seeing i.e. what I see is misleading.
what with his gust is 'greeing i.e. what he likes best, what suits his appetite. (*De gustibus non est disputandum*).
And to his palate doth prepare the cup A reference back to 'kingly' and 'monarch', since this is calculated to please.
If it be poison'd . . . begin The idea is of the cup being poisoned, and the 'taster' sampling it and liking it.

Sonnet 115

The poet ponders his former inadequate praises of his beloved; again this is linked with time, which has made the poet's love deeper and fuller. The second part of the octave exemplifies this by wide-ranging examples. The ultimate comparison is that of love to the growing child, since both increase.

most full flame i.e. very strong.
burn clearer i.e. even more clearly; that is, with a fuller love.
reckoning Time It is the poet who is calculating what can happen in time.

million'd accidents i.e. the changes and chances of time are numberless.

Tan sacred beauty Probably 'coarsen' (as when ageing skin – leathery).

blunt the sharp'st intents i.e. weaken the strongest resolve, the 'native hue of resolution'.

Divert strong minds ... things Place fixed purposes at the mercy of changing circumstances.

o'er incertainty Without any doubts.

Crowning the present ... rest i.e. reckoning that this moment was the peak, (and doubting whether what is to come could be better).

Love is a babe ... grow Like a baby, love keeps growing, and the poet feels that by saying this he will be enhancing love's growth.

Sonnet 116

One of the most celebrated of all the sonnets. It has a positive rhetorical flourish, and particularly effective is the nautical imagery of the second quatrain.

Let me not ... impediments An echo of the marriage service. May I never allow obstacles to be placed in the way of a fitting, true and faithful union.

alters when it alteration finds Changes when changes – either in affection or appearance – become apparent.

Or bends with the remover to remove Or follows the other person in his departure from love: i.e. accepts the change.

an ever-fixed mark Beacon or object by which a course is set.

on tempests i.e. great changes and crises.

wandering bark i.e. an errant ship, a ship off course.

Whose worth's unknown although his height be taken i.e. although the course of the ship can be calculated by a star, the value of that star (perhaps in an astrological sense) cannot be known.

Love's not Time's fool i.e. love cannot be influenced by time.

though rosy lips ... bending sickle's compass come Though all are physically subject to the onward movement of the years.
edge of doom Day of judgement, but note that 'edge' suggests nearness to a physical drop, thus emphasizing the nature of the final change.

Sonnet 117

An invocation to the friend, asking to be accused of ingratitude; also of wasting his time and energies on others who are not worth it. The self-indictment continues, with the poet advising the friend to add supposition to proof. But in the final account the poet argues that he has merely tried to test the 'constancy and virtue of your love'.

that I have scanted all i.e. not done properly.
your great deserts How very much you deserve (of me).
your dearest love to call i.e. to call to it, invoke it.
bonds Loyalties.
unknown minds i.e. commonplace.
dear-purchased right The implication is that the friend's love is so precious that he has 'bought' the poet's time.
hoisted sail to all the winds i.e. gone wherever I chose, irresponsibly.
Book Note, take down.
And on just proof surmise accumulate i.e. to the proof (of my wrongs) add what you suspect me of doing.
Bring me within ... frown i.e. look severely on me (but do not be angry enough to hate me).
my appeal Legal sound again – perhaps 'pleading'.
to prove i.e. test.

Sonnet 118

The poet first compares love's passion with the appetite for food, then continues with the analogy of purging to avoid illness, and the poet's taking of 'bitter sauces' as an emotional medicine to prevent his becoming sick with too much love (though he admits that the beloved's sweetness is 'never cloying'). These analogies continue to the end of an undistinguished poem.

Like as i.e. just as.
eager compounds i.e. sharp sauces.
prevent our maladies unseen Ward off our 'maladies unseen' – to use as prophylactics.
To bitter sauces did I frame my feeding This is a continuation of the imagery above. What it means is that the poet mixed with lesser people.
sick of welfare i.e. having tasted too much happiness (in the past), I now found that it was fitting that I should go to the other extreme.
Thus policy in love ... assur'd These lines mean that the poet was 'too clever by half' in guarding against non-existent complications in his love affair, which then became subject to the very ills he had anticipated.
And brought ... a healthful state These self-generated ills, at first illusory, by finally becoming reality brought about the 'healthful state' (by bringing him to a commonsense realization of his folly).
But thence ... you I have learned from all this my sickness was to turn away from you – and 'drugs' can only poison me.

Sonnet 119

There is an initial carry-over in terms of imagery from the previous poem, but this soon gives way to the familiar balancing word-play. The first four lines really describe his vacillating mood, his hopes and fears, and the next four develop this. But out of all the suffering, the extremes of mental sickness, one may find that love is even deeper. The couplet strengthens this idea.

of Siren tears i.e. tears of temptation, those which lure one, as the Sirens of pagan literature lured men to their deaths.

limbecks Stills.
fears to hopes . . . win These two lines reflect the shifting of mood.
out of their spheres been fitted i.e. (I have looked at) much lower things or people.
benefit of ill i.e. there is gain from such illness or suffering.
That better is by evil . . . better i.e. that something wonderful (like the friend) is made correspondingly better after evil experience (obviously because he is seen to better advantage).
ruin'd love i.e. one which has been debased or has suffered.
to my content i.e. the satisfaction of my love.
ills i.e. evils, misfortunes, sufferings.

Sonnet 120

A sonnet which registers the effects of the beloved's unkindness. But there is gain in that past unkindness, for the poet recalls his own suffering at that time, and feels that the wrong that he has done his friend enables him to appreciate that the latter may now be suffering as he once did. The sestet continues the theme of deep sorrow and laceration, with repentance and humility as the 'salve', with the couplet advocating the mutual interchange of regret, understanding, and hence forgiveness.

befriends me now i.e. consoles me.
Unless my nerves . . . steel i.e. unless I were insensitive.
no leisure taken i.e. have not considered.
To weigh how once I suffer'd in your crime To think about how you at one time made me suffer.
remembered i.e. recalled (to us).
And soon to you as you . . . The humble salve I offer you now what you gave me then – the salve or cure (of apology).
But that your trespass now becomes a fee Your wrong then must balance mine now. (This is a paraphrase – the sense is one of mutual understanding and forgiveness of the 'trespass'.)

Sonnet 121

The poet complains that he is being admired for his 'sportive blood' by those more vile than he. In their own 'rank thoughts' they bring down to their own level a love that he feels to be good, and judge his actions accordingly. Or perhaps, he suggests in the sestet, these people believe that everyone is bad.

esteem'd i.e. thought to be.
When not . . . being i.e. when the blameless are unfairly blamed.
just Rightful.
but by others' seeing i.e. others judge of us, but why should we accept their valuation?
false adulterate eyes i.e. deceptive and corrupt views.
salutation to my sportive blood Appraise my love affairs.
frailties . . . frailer i.e. why should yet frailer people assess my frailties?
Which in their wills . . . good The overall meaning is clear – they think things that I do are evil, whereas I find them harmless.
level i.e. aim at, snipe at.
reckon up their own i.e. reflect their own tendencies.
straight . . . bevel Upright . . . deviating (in the sense of being morally bad).
rank thoughts i.e. foul conceptions (of me).
Unless this general evil . . . reign Unless they assert this proposition, that evil lives and flourishes in all who are bad (i.e. in themselves).

Sonnet 122

The conceit developed in this poem centres round a memorandum book – probably not written in – given by the friend to the poet, then given away by the latter. The idea is that both the friend's gift and his love remain within the poet's consciousness and are there for ever, even though he has parted with the book. The couplet emphasizes this.

thy tables i.e. the memorandum book.
Full character'd i.e. filled in, written.
that idle rank i.e. the temporary one of being written in – that is, they will live in the mind.
Beyond all date i.e. forever.
brain and heart Mind and feeling.
faculty i.e. the capacity to.
raz'd oblivion Until all is wiped out.
thy record never can be missed i.e. you can never be obliterated (until then).
That poor retention i.e. the book.
tallies Sticks, marked at certain levels.
to score i.e. to add up, measure.
to give them from me I was bold i.e. I gave away the book irresponsibly.
those tables that receive thee more i.e. those in my mind, since I am constantly thinking of you (and writing of you).
adjunct i.e. a book or note.
were to import forgetfulness in me Would suggest that I was forgetful (of you).

Sonnet 123

The assertion of constancy in love, through a direct challenge to Time and the contrasting changes it effects. These are recorded throughout the poem, the vow of loyalty being forcibly reiterated in the couplet.

Thy pyramids An obvious reference back, to show the movement of time, but perhaps a glance too at the buildings of note being erected at the time.
nothing Not at all.
dressings of a former sight i.e. re-creations of what has been put up before.
Our dates are brief i.e. the length of our lives.
foist upon us i.e. force us to accept.
born to our desire i.e. we come to accept them.

Than think that . . . told The general theme is that of Ecclesiastes (Douai Bible): 'There is nothing new under the sun.'
Thy registers i.e. record of events, or of things.
doth lie Are misleading.
thy continual haste i.e. the onward movement (which destroys perspective).

Sonnet 124

Time and fortune are the themes here. The sonnet begins with a contemplation of what might have been had the friend been differently born and circumstanced, more subject to time's sway. The second part of the octave looks at what sometimes befalls the man who is prominently born. The sestet is somewhat obscure, but ends in the couplet with a call to those time-servers that ultimately die for something good.

child of state i.e. circumstance or chance.
for Fortune's bastard be unfathered i.e. subject to the whim of fortune, with no protection.
Weeds among weeds . . . gathered Sometimes weeds survive, sometimes flowers – all is uncertain.
far from accident Away from chance and its influences.
smiling pomp i.e. elevated, showy position.
thralled discontent i.e. assassination (from a rebel).
the inviting time our fashion calls i.e. people of my type are at this time tempted.
policy i.e. what is practically best.
that heretic/Which works on leases Expediency acts only with the present in mind.
hugely politic Confidently secure.
nor grows with heat i.e. does not change (a reference to his love).
the fools of time i.e. the time servers (who had been foolish to commit crimes but die for something good in the end).

Sonnet 125

This is an attack on those who try to gain favour and reputation by outward show, and an assertion that his own motives are those of love, not self-interest. The integrating images in this sonnet are those of land, estate, show and the court. The couplet speaks of an 'informer' against the poet's motives.

aught Advantage.
canopy i.e. that which is held over an important person (like the king or queen) on a state occasion.
my extern the outward honouring Public reward for praising my friend's appearance.
laid great bases for eternity i.e. set about gaining permanent fame for myself.
more short than waste or ruining Perhaps it is that 'eternity' is shorter than the time to ruin oneself – i.e. by spending all one has.
dwellers on form and favour Those who court outward show.
paying too much rent The imagery is continued, here meaning 'being too sycophantic or unprincipled'.
For compound sweet forgoing simple savour Through sophistication losing pleasure in simple things.
Pitiful thrivers in their gazing spent i.e. the wretchedly prosperous, poor little rich boys and girls, reduced in themselves by their love of show.
obsequious in thy heart i.e. loyal to you (and not to the outward show of court life described above).
oblation Offering (of loyalty and devotion).
which is not mixed with seconds i.e. which is of the very best.
no art/But mutual render No cunning, merely mutual equality of love.
suborn'd informer i.e. someone who has accused the poet of being intent on self-gain.
impeached i.e. accused – with the implication of 'falsely', and hence beyond the power of the accuser.

Sonnet 126

Hardly a sonnet, but twelve lines in rhyming couplets, and consequently unlike anything we have seen before in this sequence. The invocation seems to be to the friend (though some have thought it to Cupid). The verse is of inferior quality to that encountered in the vast majority of the sonnets proper, the conceit being that instead of being reduced by age, the power of the friend (and his beauty) has grown. There follows an account of Nature and her possession of the friend, though ultimately she has to yield him up to Time and its effects. Some have seen this as the envoy, the last and deliberate parting from the friend in the sequence. In tone it resembles some of the first sonnets – but not, alas, in quality of expression.

my lovely boy i.e. the friend (or Cupid).
fickle glass, sickle hour Both images associated with time, the implication being that the friend has stayed the onward movement in his own case.
waning grown i.e. improved instead of deteriorating. It corresponds to 'lovers withering' in the next line.
wrack i.e. the wreckage caused by time.
May Time disgrace i.e. (she wishes to demonstrate) that she can discomfort time.
minion Darling.
Her audit . . . thee Notice the imagery, echoed in some of the early sonnets. The meaning is that ultimately Nature must yield up to Time all that she demands – and this includes 'thee'.

Sonnet 127

This is the first of the sonnets to describe the poet's relationship (or literary relationship) with the legendary but not certainly identified 'dark lady'. The first few lines play on the idea that 'black' (dark hair) was not previously accounted beautiful, but since then there has been a shift in taste. The next four lines stress the fact that the place hitherto occupied by blonde beauty has been usurped. The praise of dark beauty in eyes and hair, and probably complexion, continues.

In the old age In previous times.
counted Thought to be.
it bore not beauty's name It was not dignified with the name of beauty.
successive i.e. by succession.
a bastard shame i.e. other beauty is not legitimate, not considered as beautiful as black.
put on Nature's power i.e. cosmetics adorning the face, imitating what is natural.
Art's false borrow'd face A continuation of the idea above.
no name, no holy bower i.e. no reputation, no sacrosanct influence.
profan'd ... disgrace i.e. abused, or held in small esteem (the references appear to be to blondes).
so suited i.e. corresponds to.
At such ... esteem A difficult construction, with the overall condemnation of those who, not born fair, achieve it by art, and thus give to their admirers a false impression, 'slandering creation'.
Yet so they mourn ... so They are so appealing in their 'mourning' (of black colouring), that everyone says that beauty should have their appearance – i.e. black.

Sonnet 128

A sonnet to his mistress, who is playing beautiful music that amazes and beguiles him. He envies those parts of the virginals with which her hands are in contact, and having described her playing, asks her for a kiss. It is a charming exercise, a conceit involving much play on the word 'jacks', which give it a wittily sexual overtone.

my music i.e. my beloved.

blessed wood The keys of the virginals – a square, legless spinet much used in the sixteenth century.
mine ear confounds i.e. amazes, overwhelms, my ear.
jacks Keys. (Strictly, vertical pieces of wood which held the plectra to pluck the strings, not the keys.)
tender inward The upper part of the fingers.
tickled . . . state and situation i.e. to be so touched or caressed (my lips) would lower themselves and become as the jacks are.

Sonnet 129

The opening of the poem (with its often-quoted first line) is a savage indictment of lust and dissipation, the waste of vital energy and the harm that can be caused by such action. He is 'A captive victor that hath lost in gain', as was Tarquin in *The Rape of Lucrece*. The second four lines are given over to the aftermath of reaction, the sense of self-disgust, the agony caused by the madness and self-hate that ensues. The sonnet moves to the inexorable conclusion that though man knows what such self-indulgence leads to, he is still driven onward to it.

expense of spirit i.e. using up of energy.
waste of shame i.e. a wallowing in.
is perjur'd . . . blame This whole line describes the terrible demands which lust makes, from lying to murder.
blame i.e. guilt.
savage, extreme, rude, cruel Note the tremendous single-word effects, which echo the singleness of motivation. Violence and brutal self-gratification are implicit here.
straight i.e. at once.
Past reason hunted i.e. pursued despite the influence of reason.
a swallow'd bait . . . the taker mad The image is that of a fish which does its utmost, by mad threshings, to get rid of the hook.
in quest to have i.e. in search of getting.
A bliss in proof; and prov'd a very woe i.e. happiness to contemplate and misery once it has been 'enjoyed'.
behind Afterwards.

To shun the heaven The enjoyment (probably of the woman).

Sonnet 130

Under the guise of a poem to his mistress this is an attack on the false art of comparison and ornament which poets use in their addresses to their lovers. It is an indictment of a poetic convention which Shakespeare himself practised and appeared to enjoy, and in which he performed superbly, but the irony and the satirical intention here make one think that sometimes he performed it tongue in cheek.

My mistress' ... lips' red Both these similes were used by the sonneteers.
If snow be white More laughter at a stock hyperbole.
If hairs be wires In poetic language, beauties had 'golden wires', and Shakespeare is here ridiculing such an image by substituting 'black'.
damasked Soft-textured, rosy (as in the damask rose).
reeks i.e. breathed out. (There is no suggestion of 'stink'.)
go Walk (on earth). Goddesses inhabited the sky.
belied with false compare i.e. abused by false language, imagery.

Sonnet 131

An account of the tyranny his mistress exercises over him, though this gives way to an account of other people's opinions – that she has insufficient beauty to command such devotion. The poet of course takes the view that they are wrong. He reinforces his own devotion to her throughout the sestet, though the poem would seem to carry a decided sting in its tail.

so as thou art Such as you are (presumably in physical appearance).
I dare not be so bold i.e. I wouldn't say so out loud.

Although I swear it . . . alone i.e. I tell myself that what they say is false.
but thinking i.e. should I think.
is fairest in my judgement's place In my judgement, your black (hair etc.) is beautiful.
In nothing art thou black . . . proceeds Perhaps the reference is to the tyranny with which the mistress treats him, and perhaps this has led to the 'slander' about her beauty. The ending seems abrupt.

Sonnet 132

Very similar in its play on words and in its use of imagery to 127. The whole conceit is worked out elaborately from the eyes seen as 'loving mourners', but such is their beauty, and so well does mourning become them, that the poet once more asserts that all who lack his beloved's colouring are 'foul'.

ruth Compassion.
morning Obvious punning effect.
those two mourning eyes Note that the emphasis is on the eyes throughout, and that mourning, since it involves pity, is praised.
beseem Appropriate to.
And suit thy pity like in every part Let every part of you be in harmony with your eyes which show me such pity.
foul that thy complexion lack All are ugly who lack your colouring (and perhaps her temperament too).

Sonnet 133

A sonnet which says that the mistress has gained the friend's love as well, with appropriate prison imagery in the final section to indicate the 'thrice threefold' nature of the suffering. It is rich in word-play, but the determined and elaborate working out of the conceit make it a complex poetic exercise, perhaps nothing more.

Beshrew that heart Plague take that heart (a curse).
slave to slavery i.e. my friend too is your slave.
my next self thou harder hast engross'd This is a reference to the male friend – 'you have overcome him most cruelly'.
Of him . . . forsaken The poet has lost his friend and his mistress, and hence himself (since he existed in them).
cross'd i.e. deceived.
Prison . . . steel bosom's ward i.e. imprison my heart in with steel gyves in the dungeon where your heart should be.
But then my friend's heart . . . bail Let me have custody of my friend's heart: 'bail' is not used here in the sense of 'bail out'.
keeps me i.e. as a prisoner.
use rigour Be severe upon (the friend).
being pent in thee Being imprisoned in you.
and all that is in me All of me belongs to you.

Sonnet 134

A continuation of the previous conceit on the friend, with a plea to have the latter reported to him, in return for which he will subordinate himself completely to his mistress. He foresees difficulty in his lady's possessiveness and his friend's lack of will-power; the friend was really only his surety, but he fears now that his mistress will demand the sacrifice of them both. The poet feels that he has been badly treated by his mistress.

mortgaged to thy will i.e. I have given my word that I will obey you.
that other mine i.e. the friend.
But thou wilt not But you refuse to.
covetous . . . kind Possessive . . . easy-going.
surety-like Note the recurrence of the legal imagery – (my friend) was pledged to tell you of my love.
Under that bond . . . bind Presumably a reference to the fact that the friend is also now bound fast by love to the mistress.
The statute . . . thou usurer Again the legal reference, and of course the lending of 'money' which cheapens the whole thing –

the implication is that she will lend out her beauty for interest, and there is an obvious sexual innuendo here.

came debtor i.e. who became a debtor (because of you).

my unkind abuse i.e. at the hands of the mistress.

Him have I lost . . . free I have lost his love, you now have both of us – him more completely (for your sexual satisfaction) – yet I too am caught and cannot escape.

Sonnet 135

A sonnet full of both sexual innuendo and punning on the poet's name. The word-play in the first four lines establishes the sexuality of the poem, and this is extended throughout the rest of the octave, and indeed of the sestet.

Will A pun on his own name, and a slang reference to the sexual organs.

Will in overplus i.e. you have me, perhaps more than enough (in the sexual sense).

To thy sweet will making addition thus Titillation, sexual love-play.

vouchsafe to hide my will in thine i.e. say that you will let me make love to you (again the sexual innuendo is strong).

Shall will . . . shine Do you encourage others (and yet not encourage me)?

thy large Will more i.e. intercourse, perhaps leading to birth.

fair beseechers i.e. those who would want you to entertain them.

me in that one Will Let me be one of your lovers.

Sonnet 136

A continuation of the previous theme, with similar punning and generally obscene innuendo. However this may be, the word-play is finely managed, though the tone is completely different from those of the (often) unphysical poems to the friend.

check thee that I come so near i.e. if you feel so guilty that I approach you physically.
blind soul i.e. that cannot see.
your Will Perhaps, here, I *was* your lover.
is admitted there i.e. to your bed.
fulfil . . . fulfil i.e. satisfy you sexually.
full with wills Many lovers.
great receipt . . . a number one A large account . . . a small or insignificant amount – financial images acting for sexuality, the female appetite for love being the large receipt, the number one merely one lover in so many.
untold i.e. not seen or counted.
thy store's account i.e. the number of lovers you have.
hold me . . . please thee hold i.e. physically, sexually.
name . . . Will Love me because my name is Will – but you know what Will is!

Sonnet 137

The opening lines here are an address to blind love, which has so bewitched the poet's eyes that they cannot appreciate what they see. This is followed by a play upon the eyes themselves, the heart, lovers' lies and deception. He has failed to see in a particular woman her real beauty, and the result is that he has been 'plagued' by deception.

lies Where it is – but also that it is false – typical word-play.
corrupt by over-partial looks i.e. corrupted by the preference (of a particular woman).
Be anchored in the bay where all may ride Sexual innuendo, implying promiscuity.
forged hooks . . . Whereto the judgement i.e. forcing all to be slaves to sexual pleasure.
a several plot i.e. kept only for me to use (further sexual innuendo).
the wide world's common place i.e. available to all users.
To put fair truth upon so foul a face Note the word-play, the implication being that he is pretending to himself that the woman is not promiscuous.

In things right true ... err'd i.e. I have failed to appreciate what is genuinely beautiful.
false plague i.e. the whole idea of being misled.

Sonnet 138

The opening ponders on his mistress's lies to him, and his own affectation of pretending to believe what she says. This means that there is mutual deception, but both sides are flattered by the lies, and love in apparent harmony. There is, as might be expected, much play on the word 'lies'.

truth ... lies Constancy ... lies (i.e. sleeps with another).
untutored youth i.e. inexperienced.
false subtleties i.e. the sophisticated, cunning deceptions.
vainly Out of my own vanity.
Simply ... simple truth Note the word-play, which is very subtle in this sonnet – the first meaning 'I pretend to accept', the second meaning 'straight'.
unjust i.e. unfaithful.
love's best habit i.e. most attractive dress.
seeming trust Note the irony of the phrase 'in pretending to believe'.
age in love As one gets older.
told Counted.
I lie with her, and she with me Obvious pun on 'deceive' and 'make love'.

Sonnet 139

A sonnet that plays on the courtly convention of the mistress's rejection or distant treatment as the theme of the poem. The idea followed through here is that the poet wants his mistress always to look upon him, rather than others, but to tell him the truth about her deceptions rather than to mislead him. But by the end of the sonnet he wishes her looks to kill him too.

to justify the wrong i.e. write in defence of.
with thine eye i.e. by looking away from me, and at others.
power with power Very strongly.
my o'erpress'd defence can bide (Your strength) is altogether too much for me.
pretty looks i.e. lascivious glances, as well as just her 'beauty'.
my foes i.e. her looks.
dart their injuries i.e. hurt others.
Kill me outright ... pain i.e. finish me off, rid me of my pain, let me know at once.

Sonnet 140

The burden of the poem's opening is a plea by the poet against cruel usage; he urges his mistress to go on deceiving him, using the analogy of doctors deceiving their grievously sick patients. The argument of the sestet is that if he is told the truth he may go mad, speak ill of his mistress in his madness and, possibly, be believed.

Be wise i.e. just as you are cruel, try to be wise too.
tongue-tied i.e. inarticulate.
pity-wanting pain The suffering I endure since I get no pity from you.
wit Common sense.
testy Irritable.
ill-wresting i.e. makes anything evil by distorting it.
That I may be not so ... wide So that I am not believed, and to avoid lies being told about you, pretend to be loyal to me, though you are (secretly) enjoying others.

Sonnet 141

Again the play on heart and eyes, the former loving the mistress while the eyes note all her faults. This is extended in the rest of the poem to include all five of the senses, but it is his heart which has made him the slave of his mistress.

Who in despite of view Which, despite what is seen, continues to be fascinated.
Nor tender feeling to base touches prone My physical responses are not heightened by rough caresses.
sensual feast with thee alone i.e. I do not want merely to make love to you *alone* (but also to others).
five wits i.e. the qualities of his mind.
unsway'd the likeness of a man i.e. only the image of a man is left to me (in reality I have become your slave).
my plague i.e. my love.
That she that makes me sin . . . pain The implication is that some of his 'sin' with her is expiated in the mere act of making love.

Sonnet 142

A complex opening, with a play on sin and hate and love – some would say needlessly complex – and an emphasis on the mistress's sin of loving, as well as his own. The sestet develops the idea that the woman should pity him, so that she in her turn may be treated with compassion.

Love is my sin The implication is that the mistress hates the poet's 'sin' of love, since she herself indulges in the same 'sin' with others – and if she compared herself with the poet, she would find that he does not merit 'reproving'.
profan'd their scarlet ornaments i.e. abused their beauty (by being used promiscuously).
sealed false bonds of love i.e. sworn to be loyal (for example).
others' beds' revenues of their rents i.e. taken what rightfully belonged to others – adultery, promiscuity.
Root pity in thy heart Show me kindness (allow me to make love to you).
If thou dost seek . . . denied If you desire to have (the pity) that you don't show to others, you may yourself, through your own example, be denied pity.

Sonnet 143

A simple sonnet, the analogy between the housewife chasing a chicken but cried after by her child – the poet comparing his fleeing mistress to the housewife, and himself to the child. Inevitably, the word-play (which again reverts to his name), involves sexual innuendo.

Not prizing i.e. taking no notice of.
thy hope i.e. what you want. By analogy, the 'feathered creature' is another lover who has 'broke away'.
have thy Will i.e. the poet, and hence sexual satisfaction.

Sonnet 144

At first a poem dealing with the poet's love for his friend and for the woman, also harking back to the idea that the woman and his friend are having an affair. The poet is on the side of the man ('the better angel'), so much so that the ending of the poem, playing on the now usual sexual innuendo, suggests that if his friend gets venereal disease it will be because he slept with the woman. Thus the sonnet ends in bitterness and insult.

Two loves I have i.e. two objects of love, the man and the woman.
suggest me still i.e. are constantly in my mind.
coloured ill i.e. dark.
To win me soon to hell i.e. to make me suffer torment.
foul pride i.e. corrupt or diseased beauty.
yet not directly tell i.e. I have no evidence.
one angel in another's hell Again sexual innuendo, making physical love.
my bad angel fire my good one out 'Fire out' was an Elizabethan euphemism for 'infect with venereal disease'.

Sonnet 145

A slight poem, with octosyllabic lines that add to the light-weight impression. The balance is between hate and pity, but the ending has the beloved taking pity on the poet, and assuring him that when she said 'I hate', she did not mean him – a reassurance to be taken with a pinch of salt!

languished i.e. was depressed.
used in i.e. had practice in.

Sonnet 146

The poet speaks to his own soul, the first four lines indicating the soul's sufferings within the confines of the body. The second part of the octave deals with the corruption of the flesh after death, while the sestet hints that the soul is immortal and lives on after the destruction of the flesh.

suffer dearth i.e. spiritual loss.
thy outward walls so costly gay i.e. all forms of display and show in life.
thy fading mansion The body, human flesh, as it grows older and deteriorates.
inheritors of this excess i.e. the over-indulged flesh.
thy servant's loss The body, death.
aggravate thy store i.e. the increase of the soul (at the expense of the body).
Buy terms divine ... hours of dross The afterlife purchased in exchange for the abandonment of worldly corruption.

Sonnet 147

A bitter sonnet to his mistress, expressing her evil effect on him, using the analogy of sickness, fever, his physician and medicine to convey his suffering.

longer nurseth i.e. which increases it (desire for the woman).
Feeding on that ... i.e. the body of the woman, which satisfies – while at the same time keeping it active – the diseased appetite of the patient (the poet).
prescriptions Probably 'instructions'.
and I desperate now approve I see now in my desperation that desire, which reason forbade me to have, is the death of me.
Past cure ... care I am beyond cure, since my reason has given up caring.
discourse i.e. what I say.
At random from the truth Wayward and inaccurate.
fair ... bright i.e. in appearance – and in moral worth (and of course he has been proved wrong).

Sonnet 148

Love and eyes linked again, with falseness of sight and misjudgement as their corollaries. The sestet indicates a development of the conceit, the poet reasoning that he cannot see clearly because of the blindness caused by his tears.

correspondence i.e. connection.
censures falsely i.e. condemns wrongly.
well denote Indicates truly.
vex'd with watching i.e. eyestrain caused by unhappy, sleepless nights.
mistake my view See wrongly.
foul faults The usual word-play involving physical unattractiveness and moral guilt.

Sonnet 149

A further extension of the blindness idea, the sonnet set in a series of questions. The first four lines are an extreme expression of his love, the next four given over to demonstrations of it. The sestet continues this refrain, the couplet an assertion by the poet that since she loves those who see (her faults), he himself must be blind.

partake i.e. take your part, side with you.
when I forgot/Am of myself i.e. when I have forgotten myself (because I think only of you).
all tyrant For his mistress's sake, the poet is very hard on himself. Or perhaps a reference to the mistress as 'tyrant'.
lour'st i.e. look with disfavour on.
spend/Revenge I hand out to myself my disapproval (your disapproval) and then suffer.
thy defect Your shortcomings, limitations (perhaps again of looks and morality).
But love, hate on ... blind He says she might as well go on hating him, since she prefers those who can see ... and he himself is hopelessly blind!

Sonnet 150

In the first ten lines the poet appeals to his mistress to explain the source of her great power over his heart and mind. What he cannot understand is the way her *bad* qualities have overcome him (again the play on looks and morality). Ultimately this leads to the assertion that as he loves her for her faults, he is the more worthy himself to be loved by her.

what power i.e. beyond mortal power, hence supernatural.
With insufficiency i.e. with what you lack.
And swear that brightness ... day The implication is that the poet sees falsely, and hence does not acknowledge the fine day.
this becoming of things ill The ability to make bad appear good.
refuse i.e. lowest parts.
warrantise of skill i.e. expert ability.
just cause of hate i.e. reason to detest you.
If thy unworthiness ... thee The idea is of generosity in love, and hence making some return to the poet for his.

Sonnet 151

A sonnet filled with word-play – here carried to an extreme – and in sexual innuendo. The sonnet operates on the usual two levels in this part of the sequence: physical love and morality.

conscience . . . born of love A play on guilt, and the fact that what is 'born of love' is a child – hence the conscience.
cheater i.e. she who deceives him.
amiss Error.
body's treason . . . flesh stays no farther reason i.e. physical love, with the emphasis in the second phrase that the flesh can no longer be restrained by reason.
rising at thy name The whole reference here is phallic.
triumphant prize i.e. booty, possession of her body.
stand . . . fall by thy side Direct sexual potency and the aftermath.
rise and fall See previous note.

Sonnet 152

A sonnet that deals with the breaking of vows, on the poet's part and probably on the lady's too; but the greatest of all errors is the error of his eyes, which have sworn that the lady is fair. Obviously the word-play – involving oaths, vows and connected expressions – is the main focus for poet and reader.

forsworn i.e. perjured.
But thou art twice forsworn You perjure yourself twice over.
In act thy bed-vow broke . . . bearing Basically the lines mean that the woman has been physically unfaithful, then emotionally so by replacing love with hate.
breach i.e. breaking.
misuse thee i.e. practise deception.
honest faith Appears to be a reference to the poet's own integrity.
deep oaths Sincere, heartfelt ones.

enlighten Make you worthy.
eyes to blindness i.e. so that he should not see her defects (a paradoxical way of putting it).
made them swear against the thing they see i.e. made his eyes commit perjury (by not admitting the truth of what they saw).
fair ... foul The usual physical-moral word-play.

Sonnet 153

This concerns Cupid, God of Love, with a direct transition to the poet's mistress at the end. (The conceit is developed in Sonnet 154 as well.) Here the love from Cupid's 'brand' is transferred to the mistress's eyes, whence it gives help to the poet.

brand Torch.
maid of Dian's a nymph.
dateless-lively heat Timeless and enduring flame (of love).
still Forever.
seething bath i.e. a steaming hot bath.
yet prove i.e. suffer, experience.
new fir'd i.e. took fresh strength.
The boy for trial ... breast Cupid determined to try his brand on me.
And thither hied, a sad distemper'd guest i.e. went there (for a bath) feeling sad and wretched.

Sonnet 154

A working out of the same conceit, with some variations at the end, and during the course, of the sonnet. It is a charming but wholly conventional exercise. These two sonnets obviously stand apart from 127–52, where the central figure is the 'dark lady'; these two are obviously poetic exercises.

Love-god Cupid.
heart-inflaming brand i.e. torch that kindles love.

true hearts i.e. loyal in love.
the General of hot desire Connected with 'legions' in the previous line.
by a virgin hand disarmed A certain sexual word-play apparent here.
Growing i.e. it became.
this by that i.e. what follows arises from that incident.

General questions

1 Write an essay on Shakespeare's use of legal or related imagery.

2 Write an essay in appreciation of two or three sonnets that are rich in natural imagery.

3 In what ways could Shakespeare's sonnets be described as 'romantic'? You may refer to three or four sonnets in your answer.

4 What do Shakespeare's sonnets tell us of his beloved friend? Quote in support of your answer.

5 Write an essay on the theme of *absence* in the sonnets.

6 By reference to any four or five sonnets, indicate the part played by word-play in the sequence.

7 Which do you prefer, the sonnets addressed to the friend or those to the dark lady? Give reasons to support your answer.

8 Indicate the part played by Time in a selection of the sonnets.

9 Write an essay on the visual qualities of Shakespeare's sonnets.

10 What do you find ironic in the sonnets? In your answer, you should refer to three or four of the sonnets.

11 Examine the relationship between the octave and the sestet in any three of Shakespeare's sonnets.

12 In what ways do the sonnets attack the Petrarchan convention?

13 In what ways is Shakespeare's learning apparent in these sonnets?

14 What do you learn from the sonnets of the life of that time? You should quote in support of your views.

15 Write an essay on any three sonnets that seem to you to be conventional in terms of image, theme etc.

16 What does Shakespeare specifically attack in the works of other poets?

17 In what (if any) ways do you find Shakespeare's work pretentious?

18 Indicate, by close reference, Shakespeare's ability to make successful use of the epigrammatic couplet.

19 What other themes apart from the Love theme are developed in the sonnets?

20 What do you find either distasteful or shocking in these poems? Refer to a selection of them in your answer.

21 What do we learn of the 'dark lady' from the sonnets addressed to her?

22 What opinion have you formed of the character of the writer of the sonnets, and why?

23 Which of Shakespeare's themes do you find the most repetitive?

24 How does Shakespeare demonstrate that the sonnet is not limited but allows freedom of expression? Quote in support of your answer.

25 Write an essay in appreciation of Shakespeare's ability to create vivid word pictures.